CULTURAL APPROPRIATION

The MIT Press Essential Knowledge Series

A complete list of books in this series can be found online at https://mitpress.mit.edu/books/series/mit-press-essential-knowledge-series.

CULTURAL APPROPRIATION

PATTI TAMARA LENARD
WITH PETER BALINT

The MIT Press | Cambridge, Massachusetts | London, England

The MIT Press
Massachusetts Institute of Technology
77 Massachusetts Avenue
Cambridge, MA 02139
mitpress.mit.edu

The MIT Press would like to thank the anonymous peer reviewers who provided comments on drafts of this book. The generous work of academic experts is essential for establishing the authority and quality of our publications. We acknowledge with gratitude the contributions of these otherwise uncredited readers.

This book was set in Chaparral Pro by New Best-set Typesetters Ltd. Printed and bound in the United States of America.

Library of Congress Cataloging-in-Publication Data

Names: Lenard, Patti Tamara, 1975- author | Balint, Peter, 1971- author
Title: Cultural appropriation / Patti Tamara Lenard with Peter Balint.
Description: Cambridge, Massachusetts : The MIT Press, [2026] | Series: MIT press essential knowledge series | Includes bibliographical references and index.
Identifiers: LCCN 2025019785 (print) | LCCN 2025019786 (ebook) | ISBN 9780262051583 paperback | ISBN 9780262052771 pdf | ISBN 9780262052788 epub
Subjects: LCSH: Cultural appropriation
Classification: LCC HM621 .L455 2026 (print) | LCC HM621 (ebook) | DDC 306--dc23/eng/20250615
LC record available at https://lccn.loc.gov/2025019785
LC ebook record available at https://lccn.loc.gov/2025019786

10 9 8 7 6 5 4 3 2 1

EU Authorised Representative: Easy Access System Europe, Mustamäe tee 50, 10621 Tallinn, Estonia | Email: gpsr.requests@easproject.com

CONTENTS

SERIES FOREWORD

The MIT Press Essential Knowledge series offers accessible, concise, beautifully produced pocket-size books on topics of current interest. Written by leading thinkers, the books in this series deliver expert overviews of subjects that range from the cultural and the historical to the scientific and the technical.

In today's era of instant information gratification, we have ready access to opinions, rationalizations, and superficial descriptions. Much harder to come by is the foundational knowledge that informs a principled understanding of the world. Essential Knowledge books fill that need. Synthesizing specialized subject matter for nonspecialists and engaging critical topics through fundamentals, each of these compact volumes offers readers a point of access to complex ideas.

IN MEMORIAM

I have written the text of this book, but its core ideas were developed in collaboration with my dear friend and colleague Peter Balint. Peter passed away in early January 2025, leaving behind devastated family and friends. Perhaps less important in the scheme of things is the deep loss felt by the academic community to which he contributed so generously and productively—but it is a deep loss nevertheless.

In 2019, Peter and I published an article on cultural appropriation focused on developing the conceptual apparatus that underpins this book. Our joint hope was to contribute to the debates in multicultural theory around how people across cultures as well as religious and ethnic groups can and should engage with each other in respectful ways. Peter grew up in Australia, and I grew up in Canada—two countries that have welcomed and continue to welcome people from all around the world as visitors and citizens. These newcomers, whether they stay for a short time or permanently, travel with new ideas and practices that we jointly believe have enriched and continue to enrich our respective countries. We must hope so, anyway, since both of us come from immigrant families ourselves. Neither of us is unaware of the challenges that also travel with new ideas and practices. Professionally, we have aimed in our own ways to offer respectful and inclusive pathways forward to resolving them.

Our first article came together after months of frustration with each other as we tried to articulate a view about the meaning and relevance of cultural appropriation claims that we both believed was correct. The irritation stemmed from the realization that although we shared a commitment to the same goals, we had very different ideas of how to achieve them. The result was a conceptual account of cultural appropriation that did not tackle the thorny question of who should do what about it.

Two years later, in 2021, we copublished *Debating Multiculturalism*, in which we separately articulated our distinct visions for a multicultural society. Armed with a clearer expression of our intellectual overlaps and differences, we were then able to codevelop the framework for this book, which we pitched to the MIT Press. It is my sincerest hope that what I have written here is faithful to the project we had aspired to complete together.

Peter, may your memory be for a blessing.

INTRODUCTION

Why Should We Take Claims of "Cultural Appropriation" Seriously?

After many years of discussion with local American Indian organizations, and after many years of attempts to discourage sports fans from wearing copies of Native ceremonial headdresses to their games, in 2020 the US football team the Kansas City Chiefs issued new regulations banning the wearing of such symbols. In announcing the ban, the team said that any headdresses or makeup "styled in a way that references or appropriates American Indian cultures and traditions will be prohibited."[1] From then on, fans who insisted on wearing a headdress or appeared at the gates with face paint that appeared to mimic Indigenous iconography were denied entry to the games. These changes were adopted out of a growing awareness that Indigenous groups find these practices insulting and even racist.

The so-called arrowhead or tomahawk chop, carried out by Chiefs' fans to encourage players or celebrate when they score, is also the subject of ongoing discussion. In "chopping," fans mimic the use of a single-handed axe with a slice through the air, all the while chanting a made-up war cry. Invented by the Algonquin Nation, the single-handed axe is a kind of hatchet constructed with sharpened stones and a wooden handle, and is used as a general-purpose tool as well as, historically, for hand-to-hand combat. The accompanying cry has no direct connection to Indigenous practice and yet is understood by Indigenous groups to "perpetuate negative stereotypes of the nation's first peoples."[2]

The controversy around the symbols deployed by the Kansas City Chiefs is not new. Indigenous names, symbols, and practices have long been incorporated into the names and traditions of sports teams around the world.[3] Indigenous Peoples and their allies have mounted a multi-decade campaign to encourage sports teams across North America, Australia and New Zealand, and even Europe to shift away from deploying names and symbols that are dear to Indigenous communities. Although the origins of specific team names, logos, chants, and mascots may be difficult to pin down precisely, and are the subject of ongoing disagreement, it is hard to deny that they are often borrowed—and some will say, appropriated—from Indigenous cultures.

Other teams, having for some years resisted pleas from Native American communities to change their names, have recently acquiesced to them. The Washington Commanders adopted its new name in 2022, abandoning the moniker "Redskins," a term that Indigenous Peoples consider as offensive as the N-word. The earlier name was widely understood to be a slur against Native Americans, referring to the "grotesque act of hunting down and skinning their ancestors' scalps for cash bounties."[4] The change followed years of mobilization by Native American organizations. In 2013, team owner Dan Snyder had said in response to mounting criticism that "we'll never change the name . . . it's that simple. NEVER—you can use caps."[5]

The threats issued by the team's corporate sponsors, however, worked to change the team's mind; in particular, FedEx, which sponsors the stadium in which the team plays, requested that the team change its name in July 2020.[6] The team competed as "the Washington Football Team" in 2020 and 2021 before adopting its new name. The Cleveland Guardians, previously the Cleveland Indians, also adopted a name change in 2021, having abandoned its offensive mascot in 2018—a cartoonish image of a Native American named Chief Wahoo—and removed its image from the players' uniforms.[7]

The Chiefs had for a long time escaped pressure to change the team name, citing its origin in its connection to a beloved mayor, Harold Roe Bartle, who was responsible for moving the team from Dallas, Texas, to Kansas City in 1963. Bartle's longtime nickname was "Chief," and the name was chosen out of respect for him. Compared to the Washington and Cleveland teams, the Kansas City Chiefs' name may seem innocuous—and that is what the explanation of its origin had been intended to convey.

Yet this defense obscures the nickname's full origin in Bartle's longtime engagement as an executive with the Boy Scouts of America. In that position, he founded a kind of honor society that he named "Tribe Mic-O-Say," and named himself as its chief—specifically, "Chief Lone Bear."[8] The tribe embraced the language of reservations, bands, and societies, traditionally associated with Native American societies, and adopted symbols and dances that were central and even in some cases sacred to Indigenous cultures.

When the team had been in Texas, its logo was of a cowboy carrying a football under his arm, holding a revolver, but when it relocated to Kansas City, the original creator of the logo revised it into "a shirtless Native man sporting washboard abs, a large feather headdress, buckskin leggings, moccasins and a loincloth. He wielded a tomahawk instead of a revolver and was depicted in front of the six-state area surrounding Kansas City. The 'chief' was cradling a football."[9] Moreover, the original Kansas City Chiefs mascot was named "Warpaint," a horse originally ridden by a man in a feathered headdress. Warpaint was retired early in 1989, but was returned to action in 2009, ridden by a cheerleader, and was finally retired in 2021, the year after headdresses were banned.

The Kansas City Chiefs' decision to retire the mascot, and ban ceremonial headdresses and face paint, followed many years of pressure by and then engagement with Native American communities. The "Chop," though, remains part of the game day experience—because of ongoing resistance among fans and the team's management to officially abandon it. The team's president, Mark Donovan, explained, "The Arrowhead Chop is part of the game-day experience that is really important to our fans." In their defense, fans of the Chiefs argue that while they understand that Native Americans are offended by the chop and the associated war cry, it is not *meant* to offend; the purpose of the action is to support the team, not to demean Native Americans. One fan comments, "I don't think they should take offense. . . . I enjoy going to the stadium and doing it."[10]

Nevertheless, this apparently harmless appreciation of a chant and symbol that allegedly stems from Native American culture is not understood that way by many Native Americans. Amanda Blackhorse, a member of the Navajo Nation—who took the Washington football team to court to force a name change—rejects the defense that such chants and symbols are as harmless as the fan quoted above suggests. As Gaylene Crouser, a member of the Standing Rock Sioux Tribe and executive director of the Kansas City Indian Center, puts it, "When fans scream that they mean to honor Native Americans, they are passing Native people who literally are holding a sign saying 'There is no honor in this.'"[11]

Here is an example of what Crouser describes. When Blackhorse was a student at the University of Kansas, the Chiefs were playing the Washington football team. A student group called Not in Our Honor planned a protest at the game to signal its objections to the use of Native American imagery by sports teams, and Blackhorse joined. She reports the goals of the protest and how it took place: "We assembled peacefully and we carried signs. . . . We carried flags for the tribes we represented, to show that we are proud people and very diverse, from many different tribes. We wanted to show that we are human beings, not mascots." Yet she notes that fans on both sides were angry, yelling at the protesters to "go back to the reservation" and "we won, you lost, get over it."[12]

Harms of Appropriating Native American Imagery

Indigenous advocates identify at least four distinct harms generated by the use of their iconography in sports.

Michael Spears, a member of the Kul Wicasa Oyate Lakota Lower Brulė Sioux Tribe, observes one such harm:

the drowning out and, worse, the silencing of Indigenous voices. In explaining, Spears asserts that "appropriating Native imagery is something tribes never signed on for. . . . People think they're honoring us with these mascots and logos, but they're mocking us." More generally, he says, "These images create the opportunity for white people to appropriate our culture. . . . [I]magery is storytelling and we need to tell our own stories."[13] In appropriating the images, practices, and symbols of Native American culture, appropriators silence those who have developed them and have given them life, and replace Native voices with their own. Appropriators take control of the meaning as well as use of these symbols and practices, away from their progenitors, and often against their will. As a result, "Native imagery is constructed and controlled by non-Natives."[14]

A second harm is in the perpetuation of stereotypes. The use of Native symbolism, divorced from its authors, effectively "dehumanizes" Native Americans, frequently portraying them as uncivilized and barbaric, and in the case of women, oversexualized. According to James Riding In, a member of the Pawnee Nation of Oklahoma and founding member of the American Indian Studies Program at Arizona State University, the perpetuation of these stereotypes "reinforces negative views held by non-Indians toward Indians," and leads to or at least enables discrimination and racism against them.[15] Wider society's image of who Natives are is narrowed to these stereotypes, and the wide diversity of traditions, cultures, and histories of distinct groups is ignored. A commentator worries, furthermore, that these dehumanized, fictionalized portrayals of Indigenous Peoples creates a culture in which violence against them is accepted (rather than criticized) and even normalized: "When we're not seen as people, the potential for violence against us increases."[16]

A third harm is in the disrespect demonstrated when non-Natives appropriate sacred symbols and customs, especially where these symbols and customs have deep spiritual meaning, including the Native American headdress that sports fans had been encouraged to wear. Kim Wheeler, an Anishinabe/Mohawk writer and producer in Canada, explains that headdresses are a "sign of honor and respect and leadership, they're not a cute accessory."[17] Traditionally, headdresses are made of eagle feathers, which are "presented as symbols of honor and respect and have to be earned. . . . [I]t's an act of utter disrespect for the origins of the practice."[18] In the United States, Native Americans were not legally permitted to practice their own religions and cultures until 1978, "so, it's a slap in the face to see our once-forbidden customs and sacred elements cherry-picked and modified for mainstream entertainment."[19] In democratic states that are founded on the commitment to at least tolerating, if not respecting, the cultural and religious commitments of all citizens, the adoption of Native

American practices outside the Native American context is experienced as deeply disrespectful.

A final harm of the presence of these caricatured practices and symbols is in the increasingly evident negative impact on Indigenous youths. In 2005, the American Psychological Society called publicly for the full retirement of "American Indian mascots," citing extensive research demonstrating the harms to American Indian students. It wrote that the presence of such mascots "establishes an unwelcome and often times hostile learning environment for American Indian students that affirms negative images/ stereotypes that are promoted in mainstream society."[20] Professor Stephanie Fryberg of Michigan State University and a member of the Tulalip Tribe conducted research demonstrating that simply "being shown the mascot actually lowered Native high schoolers' self-esteem," and "lowered the achievement goals they set for themselves, and diminished both their sense of community worth and belief that their community can improve itself."[21] Non-Indigenous youths also learn the wrong lesson from the ubiquity of this symbolism, says Brian Brayboy, a professor of Indigenous education and justice at Arizona State University, maintaining that "for non-native kids, it largely inures them toward racism toward native people. It ends up giving them the sense that native folks and peoples are a thing of the past or are to be caricatured, so they are less likely to have empathy with native peoples, and they come to see us as these relics of the past and stereotypes rather than vibrant, viable, productive human beings."[22] Indeed, non-Natives with recent exposure to sports mascots and other Native American imagery responded by displaying a significant increase in their stereotyping of Natives in general.[23]

To set the stage, our view is that the way in which Indigenous symbols, practices, and imagery have been absorbed into sports is not only cultural appropriation but also serves as a paradigmatic case of the form of cultural appropriation that we believe is harmful and, crucially, wrongful. We will defend this claim more fulsomely in chapter 5, where we examine the appropriation of Indigenous culture more generally and place it directly into the legacy of settler colonialism.

But first, let us offer a brief distinction between the concepts of harm and wrong, as they are often used in philosophical analysis. When someone is harmed, they are made worse off than they would have been had the harm not occurred. When two people compete for a highly desirable job, the loser experiences harm in the sense that their interests (in gaining quality employment) are harmed. When wildfires destroy homes and businesses, their owners are harmed, and when someone falls and breaks a bone, they are harmed.

When someone is wronged, their status as a moral equal is disrespected or undermined, frequently in the form of having a right violated.[24] Not all wrongs are harmful, or, at least, not all wrongs are necessarily experienced as harmful; it is wrong to cheat on a test by copying someone else's answer, but it is not (necessarily) harmful to the person whose answers have been copied. And, crucially, not all harms are wrong; no wrong is committed above when two people compete on fair terms for a job that only one of them receives, even though the loser is harmed. If, however, the fair terms of competition for that job were not respected—because the employer is sexist, and because of that sexism hires the weaker candidate, or because one of the competitors leaks irrelevant but damaging information about the other to win the job—then the person who does not get the job is both harmed and wronged. Their interests are set back, and this is harmful, and their rights are violated, and this is wrongful.

In what follows, this distinction matters: some people believe that cultural appropriation is never harmful and therefore never wrong; some people believe that it is always harmful and always wrong; some, like us, believe that it is always at least a little bit harmful, *and* that it is sometimes trivially wrong and sometimes significantly wrong. In what follows, we largely leave aside the question of harm to distinguish between acts of cultural appropriation that are trivially versus significantly wrong. For us, and this is the view that we will defend, cultural appropriation violates a commitment to moral equality, sometimes trivially so and sometimes significantly so. In the paradigmatic case of Indigenous Peoples, which we just outlined, cultural appropriation is significantly wrong for the ways in which it demonstrates a failure to respect their moral equality.

As we define it, cultural appropriation is the knowing or culpably ignorant taking of cultural symbols or practices of significant value to others without their consent, and often against their explicit request to do otherwise—an account that we flesh out in chapter 3. The accusation of cultural appropriation is generally meant as an accusation of wrong done and therefore is presumptively bad. In what follows, we treat it as such. Many claims of cultural appropriation—but by no means all, as we will describe in the chapters to come—are made by or on behalf of members of historically disadvantaged groups, who object to the appropriation of their valued symbols and practices by more privileged citizens. Not all actions that are labeled as "cultural appropriation" deserve the designation, and not all of what we have described above merits the label of appropriation; some of what we have mentioned is simply offensive, and should be abandoned in a society that aims at respect for and inclusion of all of its members. Furthermore, not all acts of cultural appropriation are wrongful in a substantial way, and some are only trivially wrong. And, as we will demonstrate, some acts of supposed cultural appropriation are best understood instead as a form of cultural exchange or engagement, and hence to be welcomed rather than criticized. Over the course of doing so, we will also defend the claim that fair and just cultural exchange—that is, cultural exchange that is nonappropriative—supports as opposed to undermines freedom of expression in a democracy by giving space to minority cultures whose voices have been historically suppressed or ignored.

Having identified a paradigmatic case of wrongful cultural appropriation, over the course of the rest of this introductory chapter we turn to contextualizing cultural appropriation debates as they are currently happening in the public sphere. We note, first, the worry that maybe "everything" is cultural appropriation, drawing on more examples of alleged appropriation. We then situate cultural appropriation alongside connected concepts, including cancel culture and the so-called culture wars. We examine the views of those who express skepticism around claims of cultural appropriation. Then we argue that multicultural theorizing has so far paid insufficient attention to respectful versus disrespectful forms of cultural engagement. We conclude with an outline of the chapters that follow.

"Everything" Is Cultural Appropriation

There is, it appears, considerable sympathy for the project to remove Indigenous imagery from sports teams. Not

Cultural appropriation is the knowing or culpably ignorant taking of cultural symbols or practices of significant value to others without their consent, and often against their explicit request to do otherwise.

everyone agrees, certainly, and there is even disagreement among Indigenous communities with respect to the harm caused by the deployment of this imagery. The presence of disagreement among those who are the alleged victims of cultural appropriation is especially complicated to evaluate, though we will attempt to do so in later chapters. But when commentators grow tired of claims of cultural appropriation in the public sphere, complaining that they are being deployed too freely as a weapon to silence others, they are typically not disagreeing with the movement to remove Indigenous imagery from sports teams. Rather, they are commenting on what appears to be an explosion of claims of allegedly harmful cultural appropriation across a range of spaces including fashion, music, cuisine, and literature—at least some of which seem silly and inconsequential.

For example, in 2004, musician Gwen Stefani hired four Japanese American singers to perform with her at live concerts as well as in music videos. They were referred to as the "Harajuku girls," named after a chic Tokyo neighborhood. Stefani has a long-standing love for and interest in Japanese culture. Some were angered by the work, however, produced by Stefani and her collaborators. One commentator, Margaret Cho, argued that the Harajuku girls reflect "racial stereotypes," and called Stefani's concert a "minstrel show" that glorified stereotypes of giggling, submissive Japanese women.[25]

Nearly ten years later, Stefani, who continued to collaborate with these singers, was accused not simply of glorifying stereotypes but more specifically of engaging in harmful cultural appropriation. Mihi Ahn, in a scathing critique of Stefani's choices to reflect and present elements of Japanese culture as part of her performances, wrote that "Stefani fawns over harajuku style in her lyrics, but her appropriation of this subculture makes about as much sense as the Gap selling Anarchy T-shirts; she's swallowed a subversive youth culture in Japan and barfed up another image of submissive giggling Asian women."[26] Reflecting on her early artistic choices on the fifteenth anniversary of her debut album, Stefani explained that her love of Japanese culture is long-standing, and that she hoped her fans and critics could see that her work is in effect "an artistic and literal bow down to a culture that I was a superfan of." She further remarked that her love for the fashion trends of Harajuku were an inspiration to her: "When I got there and saw how fashion-obsessed they were, I thought they were my people because my style was so unique. I get a little defensive when people [call it cultural appropriation] because if we didn't allow each other to share our cultures, what would we be?"[27]

Claims of cultural appropriation have similarly been launched at yoga instructors whose origins are not on the Indian subcontinent. For instance, at the University of Ottawa in Canada, instructor Jen Sharf had been offering free yoga classes at the Centre for Students with Disabilities for seven years when, in fall 2015, she was told the class would not be running that year; students had apparently signaled that they were "uncomfortable with some of the 'cultural issues' involved." Speaking to the concern, Sharf said, "I guess it was this cultural appropriation issue because yoga originally comes from India." Sharf indicated she recommended changing the name of the class, saying, "It's simple enough, just call it mindful stretching. . . . We're not going through the finer points of scripture. We're talking about basic physical awareness and how to stretch so that you feel good."[28] But the class was not reinstated.

Yoga's history is a complex one, but ancient Hindu texts refer to yoga as a form of spiritual practice that is manifest at least in part in physical movement. Yoga comes in many "schools," and is connected spiritually to Hinduism, Buddhism, and Jainism. Practitioners typically engage in taking specific, named poses to achieve a calming of the mind and other goods. The so-called modern practice of yoga, which many readers will have participated in, arrived in the United States in the late 1800s, when Swami Vivekananda introduced a reformed interpretation of Hinduism, complete with yogic practice, to the Chicago Parliament of Religions in 1893.[29] One London-based instructor explains that the difficulty is not that non-Indians are offering instruction in yoga; some of them may well be qualified to do so, and there are many benefits to yogic practice even if it is not carried out as part of a spiritual or religious practice. Rather, the instructor contends, "Yoga in the west has been so heavily commodified that 'Namaste in bed' T-shirts and tattoos of decontextualised Sanskrit and Hindu gods have become commonplace."[30]

Claims of cultural appropriation are also launched at individuals in the fashion space. For example, in 1994, Karl Lagerfeld was accused of cultural appropriation when he printed a verse from the Quran onto a corset; in 2020, Isabel Marant was accused of the same after allegedly appropriating Indigenous Mexican designs in one of her collections; and in 2021, designer Louis Vuitton was similarly accused after he designed a scarf seemingly influenced by the Palestinian keffiyeh.[31]

In 2018, a teenager set off an extensive debate after an image of the cheongsam, a Chinese-origin dress, that she wore to her high school prom went viral after she posted it to social media. One Twitter user responded, "My culture is NOT your prom dress," continuing that he was proud of his culture, and "for it to be simply subject to American consumerism and cater to a white audience, is parallel to colonial ideology." Responses were mixed, however, and one commentator, based in Hong Kong, noted, "It's ridiculous to criticize this as cultural appropriation.... From the perspective of a Chinese person, if a foreign woman wears a qipao and thinks she looks pretty, then why shouldn't she wear it?"[32]

The responses to these cases reasonably vary, as readers can see. Some find the claims exaggerated and overwrought, impinging on the normal ways in which individuals interact with cultures that are not their "own" but that they nonetheless appreciate and respect. For those who do find these claims exaggerated, these engagements are evidence of "appreciation" not "appropriation." Others see wrong in these interactions for the ways in which they decontextualize practices and symbols of the value and the often significant spiritual meaning and import they have to the cultures that developed them and for which they are representative. As we argue over the course of this book, some forms of cultural exchange are simply exchange, and other forms veer into cultural appropriation. Some cases, as in the use of Indigenous symbols and practices in sports, are clearly harmful and generally agreed to be worth avoiding, whereas others are more ambiguous, as we believe is the case with respect to the fashion and music examples we have just outlined. Our objective is to offer a way to mediate these disagreements as well as to identify when and where culturally appropriative actions are harmful, and therefore wrongful, such that we recommend against them. Even if readers do not reach the same conclusions we do about specific acts of (alleged) cultural appropriation, our hope is that the strategies we offer to evaluate the cases can help make sense of these now common disputes.

Culture Wars and Cancel Culture

Our book focuses specifically on cultural appropriation. But cultural appropriation is part of a cluster of concepts that are bandied about in public discourse, including "culture wars," "political correctness," "wokeness," and "cancel culture," none of which is precisely defined. We will do our best to set some plausible definitions here and connect claims of cultural appropriation to them.

A culture war is just as it sounds: a conflict between social and sometimes political groups that are defined by distinctive and opposing cultural values, each of which desires that its own values and beliefs dominate. "The" culture wars refer to ideological groups in Western states, divided between conservative and progressive forces, battling over social questions, often relating to the rights of women as well as gender and sexual minorities. In the United States, the right to access abortion has long been central to the so-called culture wars; more recently, the rights of transgender individuals have been central to cultural wars in the United States and across democratic countries.[33]

Cancel culture emerges in the context of the culture wars; adversaries call for the "canceling" or "silencing" of opposing viewpoints. Defined neutrally, cancel culture describes a set of "collective strategies by activists using social pressures to achieve cultural ostracism of targets (someone or something) accused of offensive words or deeds."[34] For many on the Left, one way to demonstrate respect for others is to avoid expressing views or acting in ways that marginalize, oppress, or stereotype others, especially those who are members of religious, ethnocultural, and sexual/gender minorities; avoiding acts of cultural appropriation and calling out others where they engage in cultural appropriation can be one way of manifesting this commitment. Especially in the United States, the Left has been accused of calling too frequently for the cancellation of certain voices or views that are insufficiently progressive, and recently for being oversensitive in the context of the #MeToo movement that highlighted the ways in which (mainly) men went unpunished for sexual harassment and called for their public "cancellation." According to the Right, these views are not reflective of US perspectives more generally and therefore need to be combated. Regardless of who is doing the "canceling," the objective is to harm the reputations of those who are canceled, and to reduce the influence that they have when they speak publicly.

Even among those who mainly stay away from these culture wars, there exists skepticism that cultural appropriation is as bad as some claim. Among those who are doubtful that cultural appropriation is wrong and thus should be avoided, there are several distinct positions.

One view emphasizes that cultures interact with each other and have done so throughout history, in all kinds of ways. Cultural engagement, moreover, cannot be stopped; human history just *is* the exchange of cultural ideas and practices. Restrictions on some forms of cultural engagement suppress the creativity that we have historically celebrated as central to the progress of human civilization. People travel to new countries, and encounter new and better ways of doing things; people meet people who come from distinct cultures and backgrounds, and learn from them; and so on. Over the course of these interactions, individuals gain knowledge of different cuisines they may prefer to prepare and eat, artistic forms and practices they may find appealing and wish to emulate, ways of dress that they find attractive and wish to adopt, and so forth.

Attempts to interfere with and halt these perfectly common and expected interactions interrupt the freedom to engage with others that is an everyday part of human life, and, in any case, would be effectively impossible. Those who hold this stance fear that if we accepted the wrongness of cultural appropriation, the only solution would be to grant each culture full and complete control of its cultural products, making people gatekeepers for their practices, stories, values, and symbols. Allowing cultures to be exclusive gatekeepers of their cultural products, whether they are practices, stories, values, or symbols, runs the risk of cementing the notion that the way human civilization is now is how it will always be, and denies opportunities for change into the indefinite future.

This objection—that cultural engagement is central to human progress—is not a defense of cultural appropriation, nor is it a denial that cultural appropriation is real. It is rather an objection to the idea that the forms of cultural engagement that are called (by some) cultural appropriation should be restricted or controlled, especially by the (heavy hand of the) state. The worry is that were the state to get involved in the business of policing acts of cultural appropriation, it would inevitably bureaucratize the way in which it extends permission (or not) to deploy or engage with the cultural practices of others, and in ways that would be frustrating and counterproductive to the engagement that is sought as well as the benefits that such engagement can bring.

A second and related perspective emphasizes that cultural exchange generates benefits of all kinds. Think of trivial examples like the incorporation of tomatoes into Italian cuisine when they were introduced from the Americas in the 1500s. What a benefit to Italian cuisine and all of us who enjoy it! Or think of how musical or other art forms shift in response to the immigration of artists from around the world. Correspondingly, restricting cultural engagement feels counterintuitive given that some of the best ideas across human history are the result of cultures interacting with and learning from each other. Or consider the incorporation (or imposition) of democratic political norms and institutions into previously authoritarian states. This worry is especially strong in the domain of the arts—visual arts, music, theater, and dance—which often fuses together concepts and ideas across cultures to produce pieces that are interesting and frequently even uncomfortable. One might even say it is the *purpose* of at least some forms of art, including culturally appropriative art, to make their audiences uncomfortable and generate controversy. As one commentator writes, "Art has historically been a potent catalyst for social change and awareness, with controversial works often challenging societal norms and sparking important conversations."[35] And so on this view, demands to halt cultural appropriation amount to demands to halt normal human exchange in ways that would render life less rich for all of us.

Some critics of cultural appropriation claims suggest further that it is typically to the benefit of disadvantaged communities that their cultural products attain some derivative attention from the ways in which they are marketed by those in relative positions of privilege. Here let us introduce an example we will consider more deeply in chapter 4: English celebrity chef Jamie Oliver's choice to market a product as "jerk rice." One critic objected that Oliver was able to profit from selling Jamaican-style food while actual Jamaicans were not able to benefit from the same product. But others simply assert that while it is not fair that Oliver is more easily able to profit from selling jerk, there are indirect benefits for Jamaican chefs, whose flavors become more familiar to British people, who may then be more likely to visit Jamaican restaurants run by Jamaicans. We should, in cases like these, acknowledge the racism in society in which some disadvantaged group's contributions are recognized only when a member of the privileged class absorbs them and presents them as accessible. But the alternative, in which this recognition is never offered, is not transparently better. We can fight racism and simultaneously accept that under some conditions, the use of cultural materials by privileged individuals can generate benefits for the communities from which those materials spring.

There is a third general expression of claims of cultural appropriation that is angrier and more aggressive, placing them at the center of the culture wars we described above. This skepticism accuses those who treat normal cultural exchange as a form of cultural appropriation, and therefore as harmful at least in some cases, as engaging in an unproductive form of political correctness. Political correctness, understood neutrally, refers to the commitment to avoid insulting or discriminating against minorities. But those who are wary of it claim that political correctness can stifle ordinary and harmless interactions. Here is one such expression: "We are troubled, however, by the barriers that political correctness can pose to developing constructive, engaged relationships at work. In cultures regulated by political correctness, people feel judged and fear being blamed. They worry about how others view them as representatives of their social identity groups. They feel inhibited and afraid to address even the most banal issues directly."[36] These authors worry that, for example, white managers will feel uncomfortable offering advice or critique to minority-status employees for fear of being accused of racism or discrimination.

Others are even more forcefully opposed to cultural appropriation claims, arguing that where minorities allege that something is cultural appropriation, they are engaging in a form of identity politics that should be rejected. When minorities are accused of engaging in identity politics, the critique is that rather than generating cross-cultural alliances and generally integrating into the larger society, they are inwardly focused on the needs and preferences of the group in which they are a member.[37] This inward turn among minority groups that reject integration is a sign—for at least some critics—that multiculturalism has failed. Multiculturalism's objective is to secure the conditions under which minorities' cultural and religious practices can be accommodated in public spaces, but according to critics, this project has failed and instead given minorities ammunition to avoid integration of any kind, allowing and encouraging them to live insular lives.[38]

This critique has two formulations. One worries that directing attention toward protecting and accommodating minority identities and cultural practices has taken away the spotlight from what really damages democratic communities—namely, economic inequalities.[39] This formulation does not deny that there is discrimination or that minorities merit respect; it just fears that a focus on accommodations in order to combat them distracts otherwise well-meaning political actors from doing the work needed to ensure better economic redistribution to those who are least well-off among a population.

A second formulation argues that identity politics has in fact led to a politics of grievance in which minorities have become too sensitive to criticism of their cultural symbols and practices. On this view, in the face of criticism or even ridicule, minorities should just develop a thick skin rather than cry "cultural appropriation" in response to every perceived slight, as an attempt to shut down speech that they dislike. The right to ridicule is important in democratic societies—it is a key aspect of freedom of expression—and minorities must be prepared to accept it instead of complaining that it is offensive and hurtful.[40]

Let us focus on this second formulation of the objection for a moment to illustrate its significance and then how it connects to claims of cultural appropriation. Freedom of expression is central to successful democratic politics; citizens and residents must be able to speak their minds in public spaces, often in defense of or opposition to proposed public policies.[41] They must be able as well to articulate and defend unpopular views. Indeed, these unpopular views may well be most in need of protection. Their public articulation generates at least two important benefits. One benefit is that, though unpopular, they may be correct; think of abolitionists decrying slavery at a time where it was largely treated as acceptable practice. Another benefit is that although unpopular, they may nevertheless hold sway with some individuals, who would understand their restriction from public space as unfair or unjust; moreover, if these unpopular views are *untrue*, it can be helpful and productive to have them refuted in public space.[42]

So at least for some among those who object to cultural appropriation as wrong, cultural appropriation itself may amount to a form of expression that requires protection; correspondingly, calls to avoid it are in effect calls to restrict freedom of expression. In other words, the "using" of cultural practices and symbols that belong to other groups is an element of free expression, and claims of cultural appropriation and the corresponding demand to avoid engaging in it are understood as violations of freedom of expression.[43] When artists borrow from other cultures to produce their work, for example, they are engaging in free expression as it is protected in democratic societies—even if what they are doing is somehow *wrong* (in later chapters, we contend that some ways of borrowing are indeed wrong), it is protected as a form of speech.

In some disputes around cultural appropriation, this worry about free expression is clearer than others. For instance, Lionel Shriver, a well-known and well-regarded fiction writer, expressed anxiety that no good fiction can be written if claims of cultural appropriation are taken seriously. As she observes, many great works of fiction have featured authors writing from perspectives that are not representative of their own background:

> In his masterwork English Passengers, Matthew Kneale would have restrained himself from including chapters written in an Aboriginal's voice—though these are some of the richest, most compelling passages in that novel. If Dalton Trumbo had been scared off of describing being trapped in a body with no arms, legs, or face because he was not personally disabled—because he had not been through a World War I maiming himself and therefore had no right to "appropriate" the isolation of a paraplegic—we wouldn't have the haunting 1938 classic, Johnny Got His Gun.

For Shriver, minorities are being encouraged to treat their identities and experiences as possessions, and hence experience attempts by (among others) fiction writers to portray their perspectives as "theft." But the result of taking this position seriously is that fiction writers will simply not be able to do their work. As Shriver describes the view, we are living in a "climate of super-sensitivity, giving rise to proliferating prohibitions supposedly in the interest of social justice that constrain fiction writers and prospectively makes [*sic*] our work impossible."[44] So if fiction writers like Shriver were to accept the premise that cultural appropriation is harmful and should be avoided, then their freedom to express their views—and also to create art that is provocative and even revolutionary—would be unacceptably constrained.

Why Multiculturalists Should Care About Cultural Appropriation

The political theory of multiculturalism has historically been focused on two major, related issues: minority rights accommodation and the sustaining of trust among diverse populations. Both of these concerns invoke "culture," suggesting, for example, that minorities are keen to protect their culture, in the first case, or that minorities must integrate into the larger culture in order to sustain trust, in the second.

What is "culture," though? Culture is invoked in a wide range of contexts. Countries are often described as having distinct cultures—Jamaican culture, for instance, or Indonesian culture. Religious or ethnic groups are sometimes portrayed as having distinct cultures; it makes sense to describe Hutterite communities as having a specific culture or Buddhists as having a culture. Culture is also used to cover other scenarios; workplaces might be depicted as having a particular culture or Canadians might describe a distinctive hockey culture. For the purposes of this book, we use the term "culture" to refer to the norms, practices, interests, and values that characterize specific groups—in our case, frequently but not always immigrant groups. One can be a member of multiple cultures simultaneously; both of the authors of this book are professors who take part in academic culture, and the culture of their respective cities and countries, for instance.

There are, however, many difficulties with the concept of culture. One is that no single group's culture is homogeneous; even if it makes sense to say there is such a thing as Italian culture, Italians are likely to disagree about what that culture is specifically. Another difficulty is that the boundaries of cultures are hard to discern, and there may well be disagreement about who is "in" the culture and who is not, or what members of the culture must believe, do, or think in order to be recognized as members by others as well as by outsiders. The boundary problem is complicated by the fact that "culture" sometimes overlaps with racial or ethnic identity—but not in any straightforward way. Are children born in foreign countries who are adopted by US parents part of their culture of origin or US culture, for example? Are all Americans with Black skin (and only Americans with Black skin) part of "Black" culture? We recognize these complications, though we cannot adjudicate them. In what follows, we simply assume that there is such a thing as culture, and that it is important because it matters to people who participate in it and identify themselves as members of it. That cultures are valuable to those who are part of them is sufficient, we hope, for the analysis that follows, and we do not intend to focus on *why* cultures are valuable, nor in general who is (or is not) a member.

For political theorists focused on the legitimacy of accommodations for minorities, at issue is whether there are special rights to which minorities are entitled, and, if so, by what mechanism they can best be protected. In this literature, "minorities" can encompass long-standing national minorities including Indigenous Peoples and fundamentalist religious communities that live at the margins of society as well as minority cultural and ethnic groups, many of which arrive to liberal democracies via immigration.[45] Members of these communities oftentimes have religious or cultural practices that are unfamiliar in liberal democracies and sometimes impede them from accessing goods and services that are taken to be central to liberal democracies. And so theorists of multiculturalism consider whether minority groups, whatever their origins, are entitled to specialized rights protection or other forms of institutional accommodation that enable them to access these goods and services on equal terms, without requiring them to sacrifice cultural and religious practices that they value. Permitting modifications to standard uniforms for nurses and police officers to enable individuals who wear saris or head coverings to participate is, say, one common accommodation. Ensuring that cafeterias in schools provide kosher and halal food for Jewish and Muslim students is another. These kinds of accommodations are typically justified with respect to the importance of the full inclusion of all citizens and residents, or with respect to protecting access to genuine equality of opportunity for them.[46]

Both justifications take seriously what political philosopher John Rawls emphasized: no person in a liberal democratic society should experience disadvantage based on characteristics that are arbitrary from a moral point of view, including sex and gender as well as religious, cultural, or ethnic beliefs and practices.[47] The first justification stresses that democracies are committed to ensuring that all citizens and residents are included in all the major institutions—social, economic, and political—of society, and therefore that additional accommodations may be required to ensure this inclusion for minorities. The second justification underscores the importance of ensuring that minorities can compete on equal terms for the various positions that are valued in liberal democratic societies, including with respect to education, employment, and political office.

The second major focus of multicultural theory has been around the worry that diversity can, under some conditions, hinder social cohesion. Social cohesion underpins the willingness of citizens and residents of democratic societies to cooperate and collaborate, sometimes in ways that demand sacrifice, to produce important democratic goods, including widespread political participation and support for redistributive policies.[48] Unfamiliarity can generate distrust, and successful, diverse, multicultural societies proactively take actions to ensure that it does not do so.[49] Theorists examine the conditions under which diversity threatens social cohesion—for example, where minority status and poverty travel together, or where citizens and residents are not encouraged to interact together in public spaces—and propose mechanisms by which to avoid or undermine these threats. One such "condition" is the willingness to accommodate diverse cultural and religious practices, which can serve to build trust among minorities toward the state and majority citizens. Another such "condition" is the development of integration strategies that enable immigrant minorities in particular to learn about—and where appropriate, adopt—the norms and values of the host society. It is worth noting here that long-standing minorities, including Indigenous communities and closed religious ones, may not desire any form of integration, and therefore the social cohesion that undergirds collaboration among them and a majority community has to be built in other ways.[50]

These two focuses of multicultural theory have not so far considered appropriate forms of cultural engagement and exchange, however. It is well observed in the literature on cultural appropriation, especially among those who are skeptical that such appropriation is wrong, that cultures engage in exchange all the time; cultures have always exchanged ideas and practices with each other, including big things like how societies are organized or how children are educated, and smaller things like culinary and musical traditions. So what, if anything, makes these forms of exchange objectionable? There is a preliminary answer to be gleaned from existing multicultural theory: engagement is problematic if it makes the full inclusion of all residents and citizens more difficult, or if it makes accessing valuable opportunities harder rather than easier to achieve, particularly for those who have been disadvantaged in some way. But we contend that multicultural theory has not done *enough* to consider what respectful engagement between cultural groups looks like, and specifically where engagement of the wrong kind can generate harm as opposed to good. In our view, the ways in which minorities and majorities engage with each other—what the rules of engagement are—can have a significant impact on whether diverse democracies are successful at securing the full inclusion of all citizens, in part by securing the conditions under which social cohesion can be sustained among them over time. Through an examination of cultural appropriation, and other forms of both positive and harmful cultural engagement, our book aims to fill this gap.

In chapter 2, we distinguish cultural appropriation from other problematic forms of cultural exchange, including offense and misrepresentation. These forms of engagement can also be problematic, but not for the same reasons that cultural appropriation is. A cultural offense is just as it sounds: it occurs when someone belittles or insults the cultural practices or symbols of others, intentionally or unintentionally. Cultural misrepresentation happens when someone offers, again intentionally or unintentionally, a misleading explanation of the cultural beliefs or practices of others, as in cases of stereotyping. Broadly speaking, cultural offense and cultural misrepresentation generate cultural *misrecognition*, where dominant communities disrespect or (usually) willfully misunderstand minority cultural symbols and practices, often by treating them carelessly. These cultural wrongs frequently travel with and reinforce the wrong of cultural appropriation, especially in the most egregious of cases.

In chapter 3, we turn to cultural appropriation and examine its component parts. We describe it as the knowing or culpably ignorant taking by one (usually privileged) group of another's valued cultural symbols or practices, without its consent, and sometimes against its explicit request to do otherwise. We give an account of what it means for the taking to be *intentional*, including in that category willful ignorance; explain how it is that we can judge when consent is or is not given for the appropriative acts; consider how and when symbols and practices are rightly understood to be valuable to a culture; and look at how outsiders should respond when a particular act is defined as appropriative by some but not others—in other words, when the cultural group from which a symbol or practice is taken is divided with respect to whether the taking is good or harmful.

Armed with the definition that we set out and defend in chapter 3, it will be possible to see that there are many instances of cultural appropriation, and also that many of them are trivial and do not merit (much) response. Others generate benefits along with (sometimes only supposed) harms. But, we argue, there are conditions under which cultural appropriation is problematic, and we identify the "amplifiers" that mark such cases in chapter 4. They are the existence of a power imbalance and the acquiring of profit by the appropriator, especially (but not only) where the profit is at the expense of minority groups. These conditions often travel together, but not always, and together they are likely to render cultural appropriation especially wrongful; the presence of one of these features is sufficient to make the appropriation wrongful, however. So over the course of this chapter, we develop and defend a framework that we believe will be productive for assessing these disputes, regardless of where one sits politically. Ultimately, those who reject the idea that there is a wrong connected to cultural appropriation will be hard (if not impossible) to convince, but among those who acknowledge the wrong, although sometimes find it exaggerated, it will be helpful to have a map for understanding claims, counterclaims, and potential resolutions.

Chapter 5 returns to the examples with which we opened this introductory chapter to consider culturally appropriative acts in the context of settler colonialism, specifically as it relates to Indigenous populations. Settler colonial states, including the United States, Australia, and Canada, are guilty of inflicting devastating harm on the Indigenous populations with whom they "share" territory, and are in various stages of reckoning with this past. Most specifically, as we outline, they engaged in cultural genocide—that is, the deliberate attempt to render Indigenous cultures nonviable. One element of reparations has to do with the best way to respect Indigenous populations whose territory remains unceded; in some cases, these reparations will require concerted efforts to protect and preserve distinctive elements of Indigenous culture from appropriation, including with respect to Indigenous artifacts, artistic practices, and identities.

Finally, in chapter 6, we consider what can and should be done about harmful instances of cultural appropriation, and in particular *by whom*. We outline and assess actions taken by a wide range of actors, including the state, civil society organizations, and for-profit companies, which have consciously worked to engage with disadvantaged minority communities in ways that avoid cultural appropriation. From this assessment, we draw out two principles that in general guide entities and individuals aiming to avoid cultural appropriation: respectful collaboration and equitable engagement. Our examination of these cases, and the conclusions we draw from it, offer a blueprint for understanding and mediating claims of cultural appropriation in productive ways, given the obligations that democracies and all of their residents have to protect all members of their communities. Moreover, our final chapter demonstrates that where the principles we have outlined are followed, freedom of expression is enhanced: the needs and preferences of disadvantaged minorities are taken seriously, and their voices are amplified, generating more and better speech in diverse democratic societies, rather than less, as critics of cultural appropriation allege. This final chapter thus serves to answer two connected questions, "Who is this book for?" and "Who should do something about cultural appropriation?": everyone and all of us.

2

HARMFUL FORMS OF CULTURAL ENGAGEMENT (THAT ARE NOT CULTURAL APPROPRIATION)

As we outlined in the introduction, exchanges between cultures are normal and inevitable. People visit other countries; people watch movies made from around the world; people read literature produced from within cultures that are not their own; and people participate in cultural and religious events that are unfamiliar to them, precisely as a way to learn about them and the neighbors to whom they matter. Most of these cultural exchanges are part of the routine ways in which humans interact with each other on a daily basis. Our focus here is on when this engagement goes wrong. One confusion in the discussions around cultural appropriation is, as we see it, the tendency to conflate all forms of harmful cultural engagement with cultural appropriation. So before we offer a detailed account of the features of cultural appropriation, let us outline two other forms of harmful cultural engagement that should be distinguished from it: cultural offense and cultural misrepresentation.

Defining and identifying "offense" can be tricky. In general, when someone is offended, they are insulted by what they believe is a kind of disregard or slight directed at themselves personally or at the values or principles that they hold dear. A specifically cultural offense is directed at someone's cultural practices or symbols and is either offensive to the culture itself or to the person or people who value that culture. "Offense" therefore has a subjective element that complicates matters; whether something is offensive to someone depends in large part on whether someone feels offended. The authors share a culture, but it is entirely possible for one of us to be offended by a negative statement directed at it while the other is not. As well, it does seem possible to believe that someone ought to be offended by something that they are not actually offended by, or that someone says they are not offended by an intended or unintended insult when in fact they are privately offended or hurt. So evaluating whether a statement, action, or engagement is offensive inevitably runs into the difficulty that there is diversity in how members of cultural groups respond to specific provocations, including whether they are understood as provocations in the first place. Correspondingly, we can be offended by provocations against our culture *and* annoyed that other members are not offended by those same provocations. Additionally complicating is that people can experience offense on behalf of cultures that are not their own, thereby believing that members of those cultures ought to be offended even where they appear (or claim) not to be.

The question of offense has been central to the discussions prompted by the repeated publications of Muḥammad in cartoon form, such as by the French satiric newspaper *Charlie Hebdo* in 2020 and the Danish newspaper *Jyllands-Postan* in 2015. In those (in)famous cases, the publications printed cartoons of Muḥammad—something Islam in general prohibits—engaging in a wide range of activities. The most controversial cartoon depicted Muḥammad wearing a turban in the shape of a bomb. The reasons stated for publishing these cartoons have varied; the publications and their defenders argued that they were exercising freedom of expression, and with varying degrees of frustration, contended that the kind of offense in which they were engaging is part and parcel of life in democratic states, which Muslim immigrants were required to accept as a condition of democratic citizenship.[1] On this view, the supposed right to offend or ridicule others is one manifestation of the more general right to freedom of expression, which is central to democratic political engagement: citizens and residents must be as free as possible to express their views in public spaces, and this expression may well include views that ridicule others along with their beloved practices and symbols. Legal philosopher Ronald Dworkin explains that in any diverse society that adopts antidiscrimination policies to protect disadvantaged minorities, those who support them or who are likely to benefit from them must in exchange "be willing to tolerate whatever insults or ridicule people who oppose such legislation wish to offer to their fellow voters, because only a community that permits such insult as part of public debate may legitimately adopt such laws."[2] The logic here is, roughly, that if the majority gets its way and is able to adopt antidiscrimination legislation, then the minority must be able to air its grievances as a condition of democratic legitimacy—even where these grievances are experienced as insulting or offensive. Both France and Denmark are multicultural democracies with antidiscrimination legislation, so by this assertion the publication of offensive cartoons must be permitted by the state.

When the publisher of *Jyllands-Postan* defended his choice, he explained, "The cartoonists treated Islam the same way they treat Christianity, Buddhism, Hinduism and other religions. And by treating Muslims in Denmark as equals they made a point: We are integrating you into the Danish tradition of satire because you are part of our society, not strangers. The cartoons are including, rather than excluding, Muslims."[3] At least some Muslims, however, did not understand the choice to publish the cartoons as a signal of inclusion. Rather, they believed that these newspapers chose to publish images of Muḥammad knowing that at least some interpretations of Islamic texts object to the visual representation of the prophet; they understood that the newspapers made a pointed choice to insult Muslims simply in representing their prophet on the printed page, and the fact that Muḥammad was, for example, depicted as a terrorist in one image was a secondary insult. Most Muslims likely recognized the legal *right* of media to publish these cartoons, but were nevertheless offended by their publication, understanding them as well as the choice to publish them as a deliberate attempt to offend, and not in a lighthearted way. We do not intend to litigate the merits of the views expressed on both sides of this debate and are in general defenders of freedom of expression (we will return to this issue in the final chapter), but we do agree that it is morally acceptable to ask citizens and residents to avoid offending others where possible as a condition of civil engagement with others with whom we share a community; elsewhere, one of us has described and defended a duty of civility, which asks that deliberate offense be avoided where possible out of respect for others even if it is legally permitted.[4] We simply aim to highlight that one objection to the publication of these cartoons was that they were understood as culturally *offensive*, and intentionally so, by many Muslims across European countries.

Cultural offense is sometimes confused with cultural appropriation, as when, for instance, people engage in blackface—in which people of another race paint their faces black as part of an effort to portray Black characters, often (though not always) in problematic ways. Blackface emerged as a phenomenon in the United States in the 1820s in so-called minstrel shows in which "minstrel performers, pretending to be Black, engaged in borrowed and bastardized forms of Black music and dance to entertain their audiences."[5] Although perhaps their objective was not mainly to offend Black citizens and residents, these shows ridiculed Black people's bodies and behaviors to entertain white audiences, and their portrayals of Black characters were knowingly offensive (below we will consider the way in which the persistent use of blackface is also a form of cultural misrepresentation). Minstrel shows are (largely) a thing of the past, but blackface persists as a form of expression.

In 2011, students at the Université de Montréal dressed up as Jamaican sprinters in blackface and chanted in a caricatured Jamaican accent "smoke more weed."[6] The university responded to complaints by saying that while racism is not tolerated on campus, this event did not demonstrate racist intent. In 2015, musician Jason Aldean donned blackface for Halloween, dressing up as rapper Lil Wayne and attempting to capture his skin tone as part of his costume. In response to criticism, he said simply, "In this day and age people are so sensitive that no matter what you do, somebody is going to make a big deal out of it. . . . Me doing that had zero malicious intent."[7]

Not everyone agrees, though, that the absence of malicious intent is sufficient to wash away the harms of blackface. In describing the history of blackface in minstrel shows, reporter Doug Criss observes that blackface "was racist and offensive then and still is today."[8] McGill University law student Anthony Morgan, himself of Jamaican origin, commented as he watched fellow students parading in blackface, "As far as I could see I was the only black person there. . . . And so I kind of took stock of my surroundings and felt extremely uncomfortable in my own skin."[9] That McGill students, like Aldean, (may have) had no malicious intent did not negate the offense they inflicted on others. On the contrary, their ignorance of the offense that is caused by blackface is *part of* the offense: It is reasonable to expect that citizens and residents of a diverse society know and understand the history of minstrel shows (or at least that they are open to learning this history) and therefore that mimicking them would be understood as (or after an explanation, be understood as) offensive.

It is worth adding here that it is largely the history of denigration that renders that choice to mimic hair and skin color offensive and hence morally objectionable in the United States as well as in countries with similarly racist histories. It is at least possible to imagine that in the absence of that history, such actions would not be inherently offensive; absent this history, for example, a young (white) basketball fan might want to dress up as Kobe Bryant, wear his jersey and shoes, and mimic his hair and skin color as part of a costume for Halloween. Or consider when in 1984, US comedian Eddie Murphy did a comedic sketch for the TV show *Saturday Night Live* in which he went "underground" as a white man to expose white privilege—the skit generated lots of conversation, but little of it was focused on whether it was offensive for a Black man to dress up as a white man.[10] Absent the history of denigration, in other words, face coloring to change one's apparent race does not appear to be harmful.

Cultural offense can come in a wide range of other forms too. It is offensive to cultures when, to make a political point, their holy books are burned publicly; Muslims in Scandinavian countries were offended when as a form of political protest, several anti-Islamic individuals burned Qurans in public spaces.[11] The portrayal of exaggerated physical characteristics of cultural and ethnic groups is also offensive—such as some cultures depicted as possessing big lips and others as possessing "pointy eyelids." The same goes for calling cultural groups offensive names; the most famous one is of course the use of the N-word, but Jews have been called "kikes" and people with Vietnamese (or other East Asian) ancestry have been called "gooks." These slurs operate to portray those who are targeted in a negative light, and although some people may use them only in private (for example, to express distaste for these groups with like-minded others), where they are used in public spaces, these names are, and are generally intended to be, offensive to members of the relevant groups.

A second form of harmful cultural engagement is what we term cultural misrepresentation. In general, when someone engages in misrepresentation of another, they are offering a misleading or false account of that person in some way. Specifically, cultural misrepresentation is where someone depicts the cultural values or practices of others in false or misleading ways, or in ways that humiliate or demean those values and practices. Most cultural misrepresentation is in the form of stereotyping. To have a stereotype of a particular group is to believe that members are all or mostly, in some fundamental way, the same because of being a member in that group; those who hold the stereotype believe that all or a large percentage of a group hold a particular trait, and then refer to those individuals who do not as exceptions. The stereotypes can be about attitudes, values, appearances, or even aptitudes that these group members have, and they can be positive, negative, or neutral. Where people have stereotypes of others, it shapes how they treat those others, and how they expect those others to react. Typically, stereotypes "are spread, reinforced, and sustained in society and culture by various forces, such as competition among groups, media depictions, the messaging of political leaders, and historical legacies."[12]

A specifically *cultural* misrepresentation is one where a culture is presented in a simplified and homogeneous way, as though all members share the same set of beliefs and practices. For example, in the years 2008 to 2011, on the Disney program *The Suite Life on the Deck*, in which children travel on a ship learning about new cultures, the adventures are steeped in stereotypes. They visit Rome and the adventure involves working with a con artist family, and they visit a guru in India to learn that he makes his money from a telemarketing scheme.[13] Although stereotypes are often negative, they may also be "good" in some way. For instance, where people say that Asians are "good at math," this stereotype sets expectations for teachers or university professors about how their Asian students will perform in the classroom. The same is true of stereotypes of Blacks as good athletes and musicians, or of Jews as good with money. Sometimes people have trouble distinguishing stereotypes from other forms of comparative claims among ethnic groups. So to borrow an illustration from philosopher Lawrence Blum, there is an important difference between the claim "Asian American students are, on the average, more successful in school than any other racially defined group" and the assertion that "Asian Americans are good students"; the former is a "true generalization," which makes an "accurate (comparative) attribution," and the latter is a stereotype.[14]

Why are stereotypes a problem, though, even where they are positive? One issue is just that they are overgeneralizing (sometimes this difficulty is called "essentializing"—that is, treating members of a cultural group as though they are in some *essential* way the same) and therefore people holding a stereotype mistakenly attribute a specific characteristic to *all* members of a group, when not all members, and perhaps not even a majority, do so.[15] But those who hold stereotypes of others also misinterpret evidence with which they are presented; social scientific research suggests that they will remember evidence that supports the generalization while failing to recognize evidence against it—that is, that stereotype holders can be "evidence-resistant."[16] At a basic level, then, the possession of stereotypes of others shapes how we respond to them in ways that can be inaccurate and are often unfair as well.

For example, Black Americans have long been victims of particularly negative stereotypes, ranging from assertions about their intelligence and work ethic to their propensity for crime. The persistence of these negative stereotypes of Black Americans "has [negatively] affected [their] educational outcomes, employment opportunities, [and] socioeconomic status"; they have been denied educational and employment opportunities in ways that result in their comparatively lower social economic status compared to white Americans.[17] Stereotypes are also connected to violence in harmful ways. Gendered stereotypes about the appropriate behaviors for men and women are well documented to influence how service providers (including police officers, medical workers, and so on) respond to victims of domestic violence, sometimes excusing men's violence or suggesting that women were "asking for it" by wearing provocative clothing.[18] In these cases, stereotypes prevent their holders from interpreting situations correctly, with detrimental outcomes for disadvantaged communities. As a form of cultural misrepresentation, therefore, they are *wrongful*, but they are not cultural appropriation. As we will explain in chapter 3, the existence of stereotypes of cultural groups is often connected to cultural appropriation, even though it is a distinct phenomenon; frequently the possession of stereotypes of cultural groups enables actors to engage in cultural appropriation without feeling that a wrong has been done.

Consider another example: the celebration of Cinco de Mayo in the United States. The holiday officially commemorates a battle in Mexico in the 1880s in which an army of primarily Indigenous Mexicans beat the much better prepared and armed French Army in a fight for control over the territory. Whatever the details of the battle itself and its historical connection to the American Civil War, which was also being fought at the time, the victory was treated by Mexican Americans in California as a sign that the antislavery Union forces would prevail, and Cinco de Mayo was born. The holiday is now celebrated widely across the United States, with celebrators wearing "traditional" Mexican clothing, including sombreros, and often with dancing, singing, and drinking—without much attention to the meaning ascribed to it by Mexican-origin Americans. One commentator explains that Cinco de Mayo parties frequently look more like frat parties than a commemoration of an important and unlikely military victory: "By 1989, beer companies usurped the day, using it as a commercial opportunity to increase their revenues and began to market the day for white audiences, too. Now, it's mostly an excuse for college frats to get drunk." Although the celebration perpetuates stereotypes of Mexican Americans, especially with respect to their style of dress, the main harm is in the misrepresentation of the holiday's meaning as it is understood by those whose ancestors developed it. The holiday is meant, says one commentator, to acknowledge solidarity among "Black and brown" people, and their shared "resistance against colonialism."[19] It is not "an excuse to get drunk on margaritas and full on nachos."[20]

Similarly, in Kraków, Poland, restaurants offer "Jewish cuisine" in the neighborhood that was once populated by Jews. There, you can eat standard Jewish cuisine—and dessert, at least in 2013 when one of the authors was last there, was "haroseth," a ritual food that is part of the celebration of Passover. Few Jewish people would think of haroseth as a dessert; rather, it is a food imbued with symbolic meaning. It is typically made of apples, walnuts, and wine, and symbolizes the mortar that Israelites used to build houses when they were enslaved in ancient Egypt; Passover celebrates the Jewish path to freedom. The proposal that tourists have haroseth for dessert as part of their tour of Jewish Kraków, or that the best way to celebrate an unlikely military victory that at its heart is about solidarity among the vulnerable and focused on resisting colonialism by eating tacos and drinking tequila, misrepresents specific cultural practices and symbols. These misrepresentations have elements of appropriation since they require the taking of food or traditional dress from other cultures, but the main harm comes from the way in which the *meaning* associated with these elements is misinterpreted, so that the minorities who have originated these practices and hold them dear do not *recognize* themselves in these portrayals.

The central harm generated by offense and misrepresentation is in the failure to recognize or respect fellow citizens and residents along with the practices and symbols they value. In general, recognition theory explains that it is essential to democratic communities that individuals *recognize* each other as persons, with equal rights, in the political sphere.[21] Misrecognition, then, is a form of disrespect manifest typically as a failure to treat others as equals, due to features over which they have no control and that are arbitrary from a moral point of view.[22]

The central harm generated by offense and misrepresentation is in the failure to recognize or respect fellow citizens and residents along with the practices and symbols they value.

Cultural misrecognition occurs when members of cultural majorities fail to respect or understand the symbols and cultural practices of minorities, and often translates into treating these symbols and practices carelessly or with disregard. Although they are distinct phenomena, offense and misrepresentation are both experienced primarily as a demonstration of a lack of respect for those whose symbols and practices are implicated; we have written the sentence in that way because those who engage in them are not necessarily *intending* to signal a lack of respect for others. They may simply be intending to have a bit of fun or make a light yet (from their own perspective) well-meaning joke, and they may not know or understand how their actions will be interpreted. The harm of disrespect can be delivered intentionally, in other words, but it can also be delivered from a position of ignorance of the disrespect communicated by certain actions.

In the next chapter, we begin our examination of cultural appropriation as a specific form of wrongful cultural engagement. This chapter's objective has been to identify other problematic forms of cultural engagement as part of the task of gaining clarity as to the nature and wrong of cultural appropriation specifically. What we have attempted to demonstrate is that while cultural engagement is in general something to be valued, many forms of engagement are harmful in various ways. We have also tried to prepare the ground for a more careful analysis of cultural appropriation as a distinctive wrong. The forms of problematic cultural engagement that we described here, which are often wrong in and of themselves, frequently travel with cultural appropriation, as we will show. But they are not the same thing. Let us turn, then, to our analysis of cultural appropriation in particular.

3

CULTURAL APPROPRIATION

We define cultural appropriation as the knowing or at least culpably ignorant, nonconsensual act of taking something of value to one cultural group—usually a symbol or practice—by another. We offer a normative account of cultural appropriation, which is to say that we begin from the premise that there is something at least a little bit wrong about it, prima facie. The words "culpable" and "nonconsensual" add the normative element to the definition. We start the discussion below by comparing our normative perspective with other, more descriptive views to explain why we proceed as we do. The chapter then takes up each of the features of our definition of cultural appropriation in more detail than in the introduction. We describe *what* is typically taken; how we can know if the thing that is taken is of value, and to whom; what it means to say that the thing that is taken has been taken nonconsensually—that is, under conditions of contestation; and finally, what it means to say that the thing of value has been knowingly or with culpable ignorance taken.

A Normative Account

Philosopher James O. Young offers a purely descriptive account of cultural appropriation—one that is "morally neutral." For Young, cultural appropriation is defined simply as "the taking of something produced by members of one culture by members of another."[1] With a descriptive account, a philosopher's job is then to define the conditions under which this "taking" is morally objectionable. When we say that our account of cultural appropriation is normative, we are signaling that there is something presumptively wrong about engaging in it. The main advantage of our view is that it accords better with the common usage of the expression "cultural appropriation," and therefore allows us to engage productively with current public discourse around the fair and unfair use of cultural symbols and practices. When someone accuses another of cultural appropriation, they mean to signal moral criticism—that they believe that person is doing something wrong. And when someone is accused of cultural appropriation, that person typically believes a defense against the accusation is warranted. We thus need a normative view to make sense of current and ongoing conversations about cultural appropriation. So in what follows, we understand that any individual who knowingly or with culpable ignorance sets out to take a symbol or practice from another culture, and does so amid protestations from that culture, is at least presumptively doing something wrong.

Nevertheless, and this caveat is crucial to our account, "wrongness" can come in degrees—and in what follows, we suggest that although there is a degree of wrongness at the heart of cultural appropriations, the wrong is not always a serious one. In chapter 4, we offer an account of how to evaluate whether the wrong is serious. For now as well, we leave aside the question of what, when we have successfully identified an act as cultural appropriation, should be done, including whether the appropriator is morally obligated to stop or if external parties ought to intervene, either to encourage the appropriation to stop or even to force it to do so, and whether reparations are owed as a form of apology for the wrong done. We tackle the question of what should be done in chapter 6.

Features of Cultural Appropriation

Descriptive accounts emphasize the *taking* dimension as central to cultural appropriation. In his account, Young identifies three distinct types of appropriation or three different categories of things that might well be *taken* from other cultures: subject appropriation, object appropriation, and content appropriation. Subject appropriation describes the use of characters, storylines, or themes that are central to a culture that is not one's own. When settler writers tell Indigenous stories or white film directors retell the history of slavery, they might be depicted as engaged in this form of appropriation. This type of appropriation is at the heart of many contemporary disputes. When people object to the idea that cultural appropriation is wrong, they often point to this form of appropriation and worry that if it were not permitted, great works of art and literature would simply not have been, and will not be, produced. At the very least, writers and other artists must be able to include characters or images from cultures, or racial and ethnic groups, that are not their own if they are to portray the lives we share in an accurate manner. We will return to the permissibility of portraying characters from across a wide range of racial and ethnic groups in the final chapter.

Object appropriation describes the taking of cultural objects, often in the context of military victory or colonization. For instance, British troops battled French troops in Egypt in the early 1800s, and among their prizes was the Rosetta stone, which is currently on display in the British Museum. Another example is the man eaters of Tsavo, currently on display in Chicago. In the late 1800s, in what is now Kenya, workers constructing a bridge over the Tsavo River were being attacked and killed by lions—legend says that over a hundred people were killed, though recent scientific inquiry suggests the number is much smaller—and began to refuse work.[2] The Irish engineer overseeing the project organized a hunting expedition that successfully killed the lions, whose pelts he turned into rugs. These rugs were eventually sold to the Field Museum in Chicago, where they were restored and stuffed before being put on display. Kenya has been asking that the pelts be returned, but the Field Museum has not (yet) agreed to the repatriation.[3] These cases raise different issues—in one the object is the spoils of war, and in another it was a private acquisition—but both are instances where one country claims an object that is on display in another country.

Over the course of this chapter and the next two, we consider the wrong of object appropriation in more detail. If one has a definition of cultural appropriation focused on the *taking*, as does Young, then the theft of cultural objects is straightforwardly a form of cultural appropriation. But in our view, in most of these cases, the dominant moral wrong of what Young calls "object appropriation" is the *theft* itself, not that it is theft of a cultural object specifically. To borrow an example from an earlier article that we wrote, if a tourist in India steals a statue of a goddess while touring a Hindu temple, the tourist has engaged in theft—not a form of cultural appropriation, even though the object has cultural value. Additional wrongs typically attach themselves to these thefts, including most obviously by their display in museums, often with incorrect and even derogatory information about the circumstances of their provenance or their meaning to those from whom these objects were stolen. These wrongs are not, however, those of cultural appropriation but rather the wrong of cultural misrepresentation that we described in chapter 2; in these kinds of cases, the wrong of (cultural) misrepresentation can only arise because of a prior (cultural) theft.

A similar issue arises when considering subject appropriation. In many cases, the telling of stories or depiction of characters from cultures that are not one's own is done badly; for example, they might be full of stereotypes or cultural tropes, thereby generating the wrong of misrepresentation. A novel that includes penny-pinching Jewish characters obsessed with acquiring money is not harmful for engaging in subject appropriation but instead for depicting Jewish people in terms of a well-known antisemitic trope. So here too, it is important to distinguish instances of what Young described as subject appropriation from those where the wrong is a form of misrepresentation or stereotyping—which frequently accompany cultural appropriation but are distinctive wrongs, as we described in chapter 2.

Young's third form of cultural appropriation is content appropriation, which refers to the taking of practices or symbols that are central to another culture. These can include styles of dress, dance, prayer, and physical presentation. Practices and symbols are typically reusable and nonexhaustible, which means that where appropriators take them, they remain available for others to use. If a settler chooses to tattoo their face in a traditional Indigenous style, for example, Indigenous Peoples are not thereby prohibited from persisting in their cultural tattooing practices; this feature of content appropriation distinguishes it from object appropriation. At issue is not whether the object should be returned but rather if the wrong of content appropriation is such that nonmembers of a culture can permissibly be asked to cease engaging in or with the appropriated practice or symbol, and, if so, by whom. Since object appropriation is often best understood simply as theft, and subject appropriation frequently collapses into stereotyping and therefore is a form of misrepresentation, we focus on content appropriation—that is, the appropriation of cultural practices and symbols—as the paradigmatic case of cultural appropriation.

The Taking Condition

Let us now describe the conditions of cultural appropriation in more detail. The first condition is the one that is central to descriptive accounts of cultural appropriation—namely the taking condition. In the cases that most concern us here, what is taken is not an object but rather a practice or symbol that is central to a specific culture. As we indicated just above, such taking does not exclude others from engaging with the practice or deploying the symbol, as is the case with object appropriation. Instead, when we say that a practice or symbol is *taken*, we mean to emphasize that the specific practice or symbol that is appropriated did not originate with the appropriator—not that there is none left for others to use. For example, when Lady Gaga or Oprah Winfrey wears a sari, they are engaging in a practice that originates in the Indian subcontinent—that is, not a culture to which they are ancestrally connected—but their doing so does not diminish opportunities for cultural insiders to wear saris.[4] Where cultural practices or symbols are gifted from cultural insiders to outsiders under conditions of equality, no appropriation transpires. Those outsiders may misuse these practices or symbols, certainly, and then the harm they are generating is likely one of misrepresentation or offense—but if there is no nonconsensual taking, there is no cultural appropriation. So one issue that will be present when evaluating some cases of alleged cultural appropriation is the mechanism by which a possible appropriator came to be using or engaging in a practice or symbol that originates in a culture that is not their own.

The Value Condition

The second condition is that to be cultural appropriation, the practice or symbol that is taken must be valuable to the cultural community from which it originates. The claim that a particular practice or symbol has value to a cultural group certainly can be difficult to assess. It is even more difficult to assess *how* valuable a practice or symbol is, particularly whether it is so valuable that it can underpin a reasonable claim that an appropriator ought to be encouraged to stop their appropriating. Judging whether a practice or symbol is valuable is messy as well as deeply contextual; it requires evaluating a range of considerations, and in many cases such an assessment will not reveal a determinate answer. As we will explain, this indeterminacy in part stems from the ways in which practices and symbols are often the subject of internal contestation among members of a culture. But for now, we offer five connected criteria that can help shape the assessment of whether a practice or symbol is valuable in a way that would merit a recommendation that an appropriator stop what they are doing.

First, a cultural practice or symbol is valuable typically when it is central to a culture's collective life. To say that it is central is not to deny that there may well be contestation about the practice itself, internal to that culture. Take, for example, the wearing of the hijab or even burka among Muslim women. For many Muslim women, it is central to who they are and how they express their commitments to Islam in public, even as there is much debate internally about how Muslim women ought to present themselves in public.[5] But even in the presence of this debate, there is no dispute that these forms of dress are central to Muslim culture.

Second, a cultural practice or symbol that is valuable is recognizable as such by at least a majority of its members and even by many outsiders. Muslims and non-Muslims alike can recognize the hijab and burka as connected to Islam. Jews and non-Jews can recognize the Torah as connected to Judaism.

Third, to say that a practice has value, it must actually have value to a significant number of a community's members. This condition is tricky since there are inevitably questions about *how many* members find a particular practice important or central, and there are additional questions around whether, if a smaller number identify a practice as *significantly* valuable, the greater intensity is sufficient to justify requesting that an appropriator cease appropriating.

This latter condition invites complications as well around whose voice ought to be heard or prioritized when assessing if a practice has value. Fourth, then, when assessing to whom the practice or symbol is valuable, it is important to consider the voices of those who are most impacted by the practice or symbol. Consider practices that have a clear gendered dimension, such as in religious communities that practice polygamy, or that require (or expect) women to take on all or the bulk of domestic care.

In many of these kinds of cases, the practices in question restrict women's freedom in various ways—and many women object to them, some by voicing internal objections, and some by exiting the community altogether. Were outsiders to assess whether these practices were both central to a culture and valuable to its members, they would likely gather different results if the members whose views were polled were the dominant and likely male members versus if the polled members were mainly women.

The latter comment should not be taken to mean that women do not value these practices or the culture from which they stem; they often do, even where these practices imply that women are inferior or treat them unequally in some way. Philosopher Monique Deveaux illustrated this observation in an analysis of South African women, (some of) whose lives were in part regulated by customary tribal law. In her assessment of this case, Deveaux notes that although several customary laws treated women disadvantageously, many of the impacted women preferred to remain subject to them and shift them from the inside to better protect their rights over time, mainly in the domain of family law, and to protect the ongoingness of their culture.[6] One conclusion to draw from this assessment is that practices may persist with the willing participation of those who are disadvantaged by them because the cultural tradition as a whole remains valuable even where specific practices do not. We return just below to the question of whom to listen to when we consider internal contestation in more detail.

Finally, in our view, the current relevance of the practice or symbol is another factor to consider. That is, practices or symbols that are in current use are likely to be more valuable than those that are mainly, or even exclusively, historical. It is hard to imagine accepting that the ancient Romans are the victims of cultural appropriation when people choose to dress in togas for Halloween, for example. Perhaps the reason for this lack of apparent value is that ancient Romans are no longer alive (and contemporary Italians have not expressed concern). But the same appears to be true with respect to Greek gods; these gods were sacred historically, but their religious value has declined so significantly that it is no longer relevant to determining whether their "use" by non-Greeks should be treated as a case of cultural appropriation. That is not to say, however, that historical symbols are always available for nonwrongful cultural appropriation; they can be appropriated in ways that perpetuate stereotypes or harmful images of those who are connected to the relevant history, in which case, as we explained in chapter 2, the wrong is with respect to the perpetuating of stereotypes rather than the appropriation per se.[7] This perpetuation of harmful stereotypes does not seem to be present in the case of toga-wearing Halloween celebrants, nor where celebrants choose to dress as Greek gods.

Another issue that comes up when assessing cultural value—since at issue is whether and when *cultural* appropriation is wrongful—is that cultural practices and symbols are often, in some form, also or even mainly religious practices and symbols. In democratic states, the right to religious freedom is one of the most basic of rights and therefore strongly protected. For some scholars of cultural rights, the distinction between religious and cultural rights is significant—with only the former meriting protection. However, disentangling religion and culture is hard to do with any precision since many religious practices are culturally shaped too. For instance, whether and how women are to dress modestly—a tenet of many religions—is shaped by the cultural environment in which they live. Or consider another example: For Passover, observant Jews typically avoid eating grains for eight days. But some Jews also avoid rice, corn, pulses, and so on; whether they do is dependent mainly on the region of their ancestry. Typically, Ashkenazi Jews from eastern Europe exclude a wider range of foods, and Sephardic Jews, who largely trace their origins to southern Europe, include a wider range of foods. And it would not be appropriate to simply say to an Ashkenazi Jew about their choices, What's the big deal? Sephardic Jews eat rice, why don't you do that too? That the difference is in part *cultural* does not impact the spiritual meaning of the choices that Jews make. Having said that, it is certainly relevant that some practices and symbols have deep spiritual meaning, which informs whether their appropriation should be treated as especially objectionable.

The Absence of Contestation (or Consent) Condition

Say there is a cultural symbol or practice that a person would like to display or engage in. How can they know if the culture from which it emerges consents to their doing so? This question is complicated to answer since how one asks "a culture" if their symbols or practices are available for use by outsiders is not so clear. In our view, the best way forward (although it is fraught with difficulty, as we explain) is to consider the presence or absence of contestation, and so the third condition of cultural appropriation is that an act of cultural taking can generally only be cultural appropriation if someone from inside the culture contests that taking. The mere use of symbols and practices from "outside" is not sufficient to render something cultural appropriation, in other words. Consider when immigrants arrive in a new country and deliberately work to adopt the symbols and practices of that country as their own. That taking is not cultural appropriation; no claim is made that immigrants should be restricted from adopting new symbols and practices (quite the contrary, in fact!).

An examination of whether contestation is present invites at least two questions. First, is there sustained and prolonged objections by those who hold the symbols and practices dear? We add "in general" since in some instances of cultural appropriation, an immediate condemnation might follow, which might not seem to count as "sustained and prolonged." Even so, many supposedly discrete acts of contestation will be meaningfully connected to past contestations around the taking of those same cultural symbols and practices. Second, is this contestation substantiated with culturally specific justifications and explanations for the value as well as centrality of the symbol or practice? That is, it is not sufficient for someone to claim that a symbol or practice is "ours and you can't use it." They must offer a specifically cultural account of that symbol or practice's importance.

Before we consider some examples and flesh out the difficulties of assessing whether the contestation is meaningful, let us acknowledge one initial difficulty with connecting contestation to the definition of cultural appropriation: the implication that if there is no contestation, the act is not wrong. In some cases, says anthropologist Jason Baird Jackson, groups may be "indifferent about a particular instance of such adoption," as appears to be the case, say, with respect to the appropriation of Greek gods, in which case there may be no wrongful act of cultural appropriation.[8] There may be others, however, where the lack of contestation cannot meaningfully be understood as indifference or even acceptance. Some groups might lack the wherewithal to engage in meaningful contestation, for example. Indeed, it is at least in part because minority groups lack reliable vehicles by which to make their voices heard that wrongful cultural appropriation persists. There are likely cases where appropriators could reasonably and plausibly make the claim that they heard no objections to their appropriation and therefore felt it permissible to persist in the relevant actions. So when assessing whether there is significant and meaningful contestation, it is crucial to keep in mind that there are exceptional instances of cultural appropriation in which contestation appears insignificant, but where additional contextual analysis nevertheless suggests that it ought to be treated as a case of cultural appropriation.

Leaving aside exceptional cases in which there may be little to no contestation, and where an act nonetheless remains cultural appropriation, how can we evaluate contestation for whether it is meaningful? Consider the case, which we mentioned briefly in our introduction, of a US teenager who in 2018 shared a photo of herself on her way to her high school prom wearing a red cheongsam, a traditional Chinese dress. The teenager, who is neither a Chinese citizen nor of Chinese ancestry, appreciated the beauty of the dress, only to find that her social media accounts were then inundated with messages claiming that her choice was racist and reflective of the worst of US consumerism, and that she was engaging in cultural appropriation. One message read, for example, "This isn't ok . . .

I wouldn't wear traditional Korean, Japanese or any other traditional dress and I'm Asian. I wouldn't wear traditional Irish or Swedish or Greek dress either. There's a lot of history behind these clothes."[9] Despite this objection from someone who traces their ancestry at least to the same continent where the cheongsam originates, we believe this contestation does not meet our meaningfulness standard.

There are several reasons to think that the meaningful contestation condition is not met in this case. For one thing, *before* the teenager posted her image to social media, there does not seem to have been a sustained or prolonged movement by Chinese citizens or Chinese-origin individuals to protect the cheongsam for exclusive use by those of Chinese origin as an important cultural symbol or practice, or reserved for exclusive use by those of Chinese origin. Indeed, as media reports were careful to recount, many self-declared Chinese-origin respondents defended the teenager's choice to wear a cheongsam. Additionally, once the social media storm passed, there was no further sustained mobilization against the wearing of the cheongsam by cultural outsiders. As per all of our evaluations, however, this conclusion is merely provisional; were sustained mobilization against the wearing of the cheongsam by outsiders to develop, then the case would need to be reconsidered.

Consider another example. In 2019, actress Selma Blair posted a picture of herself on social media with a friend who has alopecia—a medical condition manifest in part by noticeable hair loss—wearing turbans, with a tagline explaining that turbans offer a solution to "bad hair" or "no hair" days.[10] Immediately, she was accused of cultural appropriation, with comments suggesting that those who wear turbans for religious reasons are subject to ridicule and, worse, active discrimination, making it inappropriate for individuals in positions of privilege to select turban-style head coverings for aesthetic reasons only. In 2018, a similar objection was directed at Gucci's majority-white models, sporting Sikh-style turbans on the runway, which were then available for sale at upscale clothing shops. Gucci's advertising campaign described the turban as an "Indy Full Turban," a "gorgeously crafted turban," and "ready to turn heads while keeping you in comfort as well as trademark style."[11] Both Blair and Gucci were accused of engaging in cultural appropriation. Were these accusations sufficient to amount to the kind of meaningful contestation that would merit asking Blair to step away from wearing a turban-style hairpiece or Gucci to refrain from having its models wear turbans on the runway? To answer this question, it is key to assess whether there is a Sikh-led movement asking others to refrain from wearing turbans in public spaces for nonspiritual reasons.

Turban wearing has significant value for Sikhs, especially men. When Sikh men in the United Kingdom were invited to comment on the wearing of turbans by non-Sikh individuals, there was a mixed response. Some men responded with cautious optimism to the wearing of turbans in high-fashion spaces, hoping that this representation would serve to undermine the stigma connected to turbans. Others expressed the opposite view, commenting that the presence of fashion models in turbans might dilute the spiritual meaning of the turban, and shared a general frustration that an object with such deep meaning was being treated merely as a fashion accessory. One turban-wearing Sikh explained the meaning as follows: "If you need me, I am here for help. If you need food and shelter, this turbaned Sikh will give you food and shelter. It's about courage, human rights, equality, it's about commitment, discipline, it's about compassion." Another described it in more overtly spiritual ways: "The other reason for the turban is to protect the spiritual centre on top of the head so that it doesn't get damaged in any way. When I meditate with my turban on my head, I feel happy and very good, the turban concentrates those happy feelings."[12] Specifically in response to Gucci's choice, one Sikh organization stated, "The turban is not just an accessory to monetize; it's a religious article of faith that millions of Sikhs view as sacred. Many find this cultural appropriation inappropriate, since those wearing the turban just for fashion will not appreciate its deep religious significance."[13] Responding to Blair, a commentator said, "White people have scorned Sikhs for hundreds of years, and now we wanna appropriate and make it trendy?"[14] So some Sikh men (but not all) do feel uncomfortable with the commercialization or use of turbans by non-Sikhs.

Is that discomfort sufficient to warrant claims that Blair or those involved in the fashion industry are engaging in harmful cultural appropriation, however? In defending herself, Blair first said, "Covering one's head is not appropriating anything."[15] But then she also explained that she is living with multiple sclerosis, which, like alopecia, has hair loss as a side effect, and asked her critics, "What do you want a woman with no hair to wear? Just an itchy wig?"[16] Our sense is that the contestation, while real, is not substantial enough for us to join the calls for Blair to cease wearing a turban as her health-related mitigating factors do seem to provide sufficient justification for her interest in considering alternative head coverings. Had she been wearing a turban in solidarity with a friend suffering from illness-connected hair loss, there too it seems that there is no substantial case for suggesting she is engaging in wrongful behavior.

What about when fashion models wear turbans? The worry that fashion models who wear turbans somehow dilute the meaning of turbans for those who wear them for spiritual reasons is weak since it is not immediately clear why someone else's choice to wear a turban would impact the meaning an individual Sikh might ascribe to it (though it might dilute the performative element of turban wearing if turban wearing were not a reliable indicator of someone who is committed to Sikh values and principles). It is hard to adjudicate the proposal that seeing turbans in high fashion will undermine stigma for those who wear it for spiritual reasons, and as we suggest in the next chapter, there are questions to be asked where outsiders to a culture profit in some way from the cultural products and symbols of others, as Gucci does in this case. An initial assessment indicates that this contestation may well be sufficient to recommend that turbans must be protected from appropriation by others.

These examples demonstrate the difficulty posed by the fact of group heterogeneity, minority or otherwise. All groups, including minority ones, are heterogeneous in the sense that their members have a diversity of positions in general and with respect to specific acts of (alleged) cultural appropriation. This heterogeneity raises at least two questions. One issue is around the question of how to delineate the boundaries of a particular group to identify whether someone is an insider or outsider; political philosophers describe this question as the "boundary problem." The boundaries of all cultural groups are porous, with members moving in and out of identifying with the group more and less strongly over time. Additionally, among those who identify as members of a particular group, there is a wide variety of ways in which that identity is expressed along with a wide variety of interpretations of which practices, symbols, and values are essential to the group's identity. This internal diversity makes it hard for outsiders to know how to read a group's perspective.

One deceptively simple response is offered in an advice column: "Go to an appropriate representative of the culture to ask."[17] Where society is divided into groups of any kind (religious, political, cultural, etc.), it can seem to make sense to defer to group representatives in trying to understand the preferences of that group. Finding such a "representative" can be tricky, though, because most cultures have more than one representative, and even relatively tight-knit cultures are sufficiently heterogeneous that it should be expected that their members will respond to potential acts of cultural appropriation differently. For instance, when the Met Gala chose a Catholic theme for its annual event in 2018, it had secured consent directly from the Vatican to do so and even collaborated with the Vatican in key ways to produce the event. Yet not all Catholics were comfortable with that choice, arguing that the so-called Heavenly Bodies event was an example of "religious appropriation"; one social media commentator wrote, "My religion is not your costume."[18] The question of what counts as consent, and who can give it, will emerge again in chapter 5, where we consider appropriation from Indigenous cultures in more detail.

Philosopher Rebecca Tuvel expresses the difficulty of going forward, absent a single clear and legitimate group representative, when contestation claims are made by some but not all members of a cultural group: "If contestation is voiced on behalf of some cultural members, but not others, do we simply attribute the former more weight? Why think claims against use should be granted more weight than claims that permit use? And which cultural members' contestation matters? Only those who are locally present, or those who post their opinions online? If so, why?"[19] A corresponding worry is that where outsiders are searching for a cohesive group that expresses a singular perspective, sometimes the viewpoint they hear is either of a vocal minority *or* a specific subsection of a group. Philosophers C. Thi Nguyen and Matthew Strohl write that in these cases, a commitment to "claim deference"—the idea that in general, dominant communities should defer to the wishes of minority cultural groups in identifying whether an act counts as cultural appropriation—does "not appropriately respect the agency of group members who disagree with appropriation claimants."[20] This worry is especially strong where the appropriation claimants are a minority within a particular cultural group.

Even more challenging, the vocal minority may be one that is not only unrepresentative of a group's perspective in general but perhaps also an especially conservative subsection of the group that emerges as the group's (alleged) voice. This variation on the dangers of the claim deference argument surfaces in feminist critiques of cultural group protection. According to this worry, "Claim deference effectively affords the most restrictive voices within a group the power to overrule the rest of the group, and thereby objectionably limits the agency of group members who do not share the most restrictive viewpoint." So, for example, in Orthodox Jewish communities, the leaders are often older men who make decisions on behalf of the entire group, but those decisions either may not reflect what the group desires in general or be detrimental to the autonomy of women and children internal to the group. So where majority groups consider the views of this community, the views that are taken to be representative are not in fact representative in a democratic sense. In both of these variations, say Thi Nguyen and Stroll, "deferring to appropriation claims without attending to dissenting voices discounts the agency of a great many legitimate stakeholders."[21]

These difficulties are further exacerbated because many cultural groups, whether internally heterogeneous or not, do not possess collective decision-making procedures to generate—from the perspective of that group or that of outsiders trying to interpret a group's specific position—an all-things-considered judgment that outsiders can treat as the group position on a specific act of (alleged) cultural appropriation. One dilemma this absence of collective decision-making generates is that where there are multiple voices claiming to represent a group, it is hard for outsiders to know to whom to listen. A variation of this difficulty is that where outsiders seek someone from a specific community from whom to get permission—seeking permission from disadvantaged groups is one possible remedy to at least some forms of cultural appropriation, which we will consider in the final chapter of the book—outsiders can engage in a kind of "approval shopping" among representatives to find ones who will extend the permission that is sought.[22]

Consider this example of internal disagreement. In 2015, the Boston Museum of Fine Arts (MFA) was running an event it had called "Kimono Wednesdays." The point was to engage visitors with a particular piece of art (in line with a general attempt to engage visitors creatively with art)—in this case, Claude Monet's painting *La Japonaise*, which featured Monet's wife in a bright-red kimono. Kimonos have long been an "unmistakable marker of Japanese culture."[23] On Kimono Wednesdays, visitors were invited to try on a red kimono like the one in the painting, take pictures of themselves with the painting, and then tag themselves on social media platforms; the appropriation was in the form of non-Japanese (or even non-Asian) individuals donning the kimono for the benefit of social media. The kimono that was available for trying on was prepared by a kimono artist in Kyoto. A representative of the MFA described the objective as follows: "The idea was to give visitors a 'tactile experience' with the kimonos made in Japan 'to understand and experience the painting in a new way.'"[24]

Critics, however, objected to the display, arguing that it was a clear example of cultural appropriation that propagated racist stereotypes of Asian individuals.[25] One protester explained, "I'm not pro the kimono being used as a kind of fetish item or as a way of glorifying white beauty. . . . The kimono, it's stripped of its cultural context. That's what I'm protesting against."[26] The context, alleged the protesters, is one in which Asian Americans continue to experience racism and discrimination in US society. Others situated the exhibit in a broader context of who is permitted to represent minority culture, contending that celebrating the way in which Monet depicted Asians serves to contribute to the often one-dimensional characterization of Asian individuals in public discourse and media. If one were attentive to the initial protesters, one might believe that they represented the view of at least a significant number of people in the United States with Asian or Japanese ancestry.

Yet a near immediate counterprotest emerged, with participants self-identifying as of Japanese origin and stating that they were not offended by the exhibit. One scholar examining the controversy remarked that the number of individuals objecting to the MFA exhibit was "a small but vocal protest group made up primarily of Asian Americans." She observed similarly that the exhibit toured in Kyoto and Tokyo before landing in Boston, where similar kimonos were available for trying on, and "no one, it seems, was in the least bit offended."[27] Not only does Japanese culture celebrate the kimono, according to Valk, "Japanese people hardly ever reject the idea of a non-Japanese person wearing one," and on the contrary often celebrate it.[28] For example, the deputy consul general of Japan in Boston seemed surprised by the protests and said, "We actually do not quite understand what their point of protest is. . . . We tried to listen to those people who are protesting, but we think together with the MFA we should encourage that Japanese culture be appreciated in a positive way."[29]

Initially, the MFA chose to defend its choice to have visitors engage with Monet's painting as planned. In the end, though, the museum opted to cancel Kimono Wednesdays and apologized for the harm it caused in running it in the first place.

What the controversy demonstrates is the difficulty of assessing *whom* to listen to and who can be understood as offering an authoritative interpretation of specific acts of (alleged) cultural appropriation. Japanese Americans, or Asian Americans, cannot possibly be understood to speak with one unified voice—and although the initial protesters suggested that they spoke on behalf of the entire group, implying that all members have the same or overlapping experiences and perspectives, it was neither the case that the protesters spoke for the entire group nor that the entire group had the same set of experiences and perspectives. In an explanation at a panel focused on how the MFA can avoid insulting other cultures in the future, one scholar asserted, "There's nothing inherently racist about putting on a kimono and playing, but it's part of a long racist history," which has to be acknowledged.[30] (Readers can likely see the analogy with the use of blackface, which may not be inherently wrong but rather is certainly wrong because of its connection to a long and racist history.) It is not, to our mind, obvious whether the MFA ought to have proceeded despite the protesters, nor whether its decision was the appropriate one in the context. What does emerge is the importance—which the MFA acknowledged as it explained its choice to cancel Kimono Wednesdays—of engaging widely with members of minority cultural groups to form a more expansive sense of how certain exhibits might be received and how best to present them.

The Knowledge or Culpable Ignorance Condition

The final condition for designating an act as cultural appropriation is that the appropriator ought to know that they are taking a symbol or practice that is of value to others for their own personal use. How might a would-be appropriator know that the symbol or practice is valuable to others in such a way that they would prefer it is not used by the appropriator? One way is that members of that culture contest the appropriation, as we have described above.

Often in practice, an appropriator engages knowingly in the taking of cultural symbols and practices and then when accused of cultural appropriation, resists the idea that they are doing something wrong or blameworthy. For example, some of those accused of cultural appropriation argue that their taking should be understood as respectful cultural *appreciation* rather than appropriation, or sometimes accuse cultural minorities of being too sensitive.[31]

Sometimes, though, an appropriator *ought* to know that a symbol or practice is of significance to a specific culture but simply does not. In these cases, an appropriator may be ignorant of what they ought to know, yet they are *culpably* so and can still reasonably be held responsible for the harm that the appropriation generates, even if they can truthfully claim that they did not know how the action would be understood and did not intend to harm others. Many of these cases arise in situations where people in positions of privilege unknowingly or unthinkingly borrow symbols or practices from marginalized cultures. Leaving aside for now whether the wearing of cornrows by white people in the United States is wrongful (we will consider this question in the next chapter), and if it is, how wrongful it may be, a key *objection* from African Americans is that the history of cornrows is not one that white wearers are likely to be familiar with, and, moreover, the difficulties that Black people have in "wearing" their culture in public are not acknowledged. White people *ought* to know this history, but perhaps do not, and their choice to wear cornrows is made in ignorance of that history.

One explanation for why white people are not attentive to the harms they do to Black people by borrowing aspects of their culture lies in what has been called "white ignorance." When we say that someone is ignorant, we are saying that they do not possess some key knowledge or information, or that they lack understanding or education in some important area. White ignorance refers to the ways in which many white people are seemingly unaware of how existing institutional structures disadvantage minorities in unjust ways, and their corresponding inattention to or dismissal of the challenges that they thereby face.

More specifically, the structures that govern society not only perpetuate white privilege but also operate so as to mask the ways in which they do so. The result is that whites are genuinely ignorant of the basic facts of racial privilege, such as that Black people on average earn less than whites do, are less likely to be granted a mortgage, are more likely to be treated harshly by the criminal justice system, and so on.[32] As philosopher Charles Mills explains, some individuals are straightforwardly racist, believing white people to be superior to racial minorities including Black people. Others systematically downplay racism and its impacts, ignoring "the visible consequences of white supremacy in our time," and instead "portray racism as exceptional rather than structural, minimise its effects, or deny its existence altogether."[33] For yet others, the ignorance stems from "the social suppression of the pertinent knowledge. . . . So white ignorance need not always be based on bad faith."[34]

From the perspective of cultural appropriation, then, many of those who borrow from—that is, appropriate—Black culture do not see that they are doing so from a position of privilege that is structurally sustained, which gives them the power to do this borrowing without consultation, and without concern that it is insulting, frustrating, or otherwise angering to and disrespectful of Black citizens. The structural account (which we elaborate in the next chapter in some detail) does not absolve appropriators from their responsibility for their actions, but it explains the source of their ignorance and emphasizes that there are many fronts on which a battle against wrongful appropriation must take place. When appropriators simply did not know they were engaging in appropriation, a claim of culpable ignorance can briefly shield an appropriator from allegations that they have done wrong. So long as they respond to such claims by withdrawing from the relevant practice or symbol, they are not perpetuating wrongful cultural appropriation.

To sum up: Cultural appropriation is defined by four features, which we have articulated in some detail over the course of this chapter. These are the taking condition, the

Many acts of claimed cultural appropriation are, if wrong, only minorly so, and unlikely to warrant much criticism and certainly not intervention.

value condition, the contestation (consent) condition, and, finally, the knowledge or culpable ignorance condition. These conditions must be met, in our view, for an act to be defined as cultural appropriation. But, and this caveat is crucial, although we have built and defended a normative rather than merely descriptive view of cultural appropriation—which therefore implies that acts of appropriation are prima facie wrong—we have not yet offered an account of how wrong such actions are. And as we think should be clear from what we have offered so far, many acts of claimed cultural appropriation are, if wrong, only minorly so, and unlikely to warrant much criticism and certainly not intervention. In the next chapter, we consider the conditions under which acts of cultural appropriation can be wrongful in ways that merit more serious criticism.

4

AMPLIFIERS

In chapter 3, we defined cultural appropriation and outlined its key features. The definition we offered—the knowing or at least culpably ignorant, nonconsensual taking of cultural symbols or practices that are of value to another, distinct cultural group—is broad. As a result, it encompasses many interactions between cultures, many trivial seeming, not all of which feel like they merit the negative connotation that accusations of cultural appropriation typically carry. For example, the choice by citizens in African countries to wear Western-style suits in professional environments might count as cultural appropriation on our definition, but it does not immediately raise alarm bells. Where a disadvantaged group borrows from the dominant group, it does not appear to be a case of harmful cultural appropriation, nor indeed when comparatively well-off groups engage with each other's cultural artifacts.

So one possibility is that cultural engagement is only (and perhaps always) *appropriative* where the appropriation is by dominant communities and related to cultural symbols and practices that belong to, or are characteristic of, minority communities. But this view is not the one we defend. Consider cases in which European chefs experiment with spices and flavors that stem from non-Western countries or minority communities, or even when people from one culture open a restaurant serving food that is central to another. Here, there is a form of appropriation, and is it *by* a dominant group of a practice or culture that stems from a minority community, but it is not straightforwardly wrong. No one wants to live in a world in which spices or flavors are restricted to the culture from which they originate!

Describing cases like these as cultural appropriation—where the associated connotation is negative, but where the taking generates widely recognized goods, like culinary cross-pollination, or is done by nondominant communities—is what propels at least some commentators to dismiss cultural appropriation claims as silly. In fact, we agree that many cases of cultural appropriation seem quite trivial; that they are trivial does not make them less of an example of cultural appropriation, however. We agree with philosopher Erich Hatala Matthes that, in general, especially objectionable acts of cultural appropriation will be accompanied by what he terms "oppressive conditions" and what we instead describe as amplifiers.[1]

Yet unlike Matthes, who builds into his account of cultural appropriation the requirement of oppressive conditions, we adopt the broad definition outlined just above, and propose that we can distinguish between trivial and morally problematic forms of cultural appropriation. Our normative account, as we discussed in chapter 3, begins with the presumption that every act of cultural appropriation is wrong. Here we aim to demonstrate that there are certain factors that, when present, amplify the wrong of cultural appropriation. These amplifiers are the presence of a power imbalance between the appropriator and the community from which a practice or symbol is taken; and the acquiring of profit by the appropriator either at the expense of the minority cultural community from which the practice or symbol is taken or without attention to the penalties that the minority community has faced historically for engaging in that practice or symbol.

In our view, the presence of either of these amplifiers renders the appropriation especially wrongful—that is, meriting of critique and possibly other action. The presence of both amplifiers renders an act of appropriation *more* wrongful than if only one is present. While some have already lost patience with all claims of cultural appropriation, we aim to show how a focus on these amplifiers can help to distinguish between significant and trivial instances of cultural appropriation. We proceed in two sections, the first focused on power imbalances, and the second focused on the acquisition of profit by appropriators.

The Presence of Power Imbalances

Where cultural appropriation happens, it is the taking of a symbol or practice from one culture by an individual or group of another culture. The taking happens, in other words, *across* cultures, and it is appropriation whether or not there is a power imbalance, although as we will demonstrate, where there is such an imbalance, the likelihood that the appropriation is wrongful is high. The meaning of "power" is contested; some people define it in terms of a person or group being able to get others to do what they want, and others understand it as an individual's capacity to get what they, themselves want, such as in terms of "power to-do something." When scholars are describing power imbalances specifically (rather than power itself), usually what is being portrayed is a relation of domination or oppression, where one group has an "unjust or illegitimate power-over relation" with another.[2] What that means in practice is that one group has the capacity to shape the political, economic, and social spaces according to its own preferences and needs, without much attention to how other groups might respond, and in ways that may well put those other groups at a disadvantage in various contexts. For example, when predominantly Christian societies organize calendars around Christmas and Easter, without attention to what religious minorities might prefer or how they might respond, and without *needing* to consider in any detail how they might respond, they are exercising their power—as the dominant social group—in ways that will be perceived to be unjust or illegitimate by those who have no choice but to go along with the decisions that are made.

In most democratic societies, the basic institutions are riddled with structural injustice—that is, injustice is built into them.[3] These injustices, which are created by no one individual in particular—meaning no individual is responsible, alone, for generating the injustice even if they participate in these unjust structures—entrench power imbalances from which only some communities or people benefit. Iris Marion Young, who brought the concept of structural injustice into the center of political theory, writes that "structural injustice occurs as a consequence of many individuals and institutions acting to pursue their particular goals, interests, for the most part within the limits of accepted rules and norms."[4] These institutions perpetuate conditions under which some individuals and groups have more power than others. These others are variously depicted in the social science literature as "dominated," "marginalized," and "oppressed."

In what follows, we use the term "disadvantaged" to capture the various ways in which minority groups might find themselves to have less power than others in a democratic society, and therefore to be at risk of domination, oppression, or marginalization. The term "disadvantage" is borrowed from the work of political philosophers Jonathan Wolff and Avner de-Shalit, who use it in a pluralistic way to identify the dimensions along which an individual or group might do less well than others: Disadvantaged individuals or groups may have less money or political power, have less access to educational or employment opportunities, be more susceptible to crime or public ridicule, and so on.[5] Many minority groups are disadvantaged along multiple dimensions.

As we indicated earlier, Matthes's interpretation of cultural appropriation connects it necessarily to the presence of power imbalances: "The wrong of cultural appropriation is rooted in imbalances of power."[6] Or as researcher Denise Cuthbert argues, it is the fact of "differential power" that "makes some exchanges but not others appropriative."[7]

But this way of explaining what cultural appropriation is does not seem quite right. Law professor Mathias Siems explains why, using the language of thievery to capture the intuition. Theft is theft, regardless of whether the thief is wealthy or poor.[8] We may have more empathy for a poorer person who steals from a wealthier person; we may feel that it is *less* wrong than theft in the other direction, both because it is motivated perhaps by hunger or other deprivation and because the wealthier person can weather (at least some) theft before they experience harm as a result. The same is true of cultural appropriation, which can be understood as a kind of theft of a cultural practice or symbol: Appropriation is wrong regardless of who the appropriator is, but where there is a power imbalance, it is more wrongful when the appropriation is carried out by an individual or group that is in a more powerful position. Why would this be?

By analogy it is more wrongful, at least in part, because comparatively speaking, those in a dominant position are less vulnerable to the harms of cultural appropriation. Why? Those who are privileged see their culture built into as well as reflected back by their local political and social institutions, and therefore do not need to actively protect and preserve valuable practices and symbols from misuse and disrespect by others. Minority groups often feel otherwise, believing that their distinctive culture is more vulnerable to erosion in the face of dominant cultures, including via cultural appropriation. So, and following Siems, while power imbalances are not part of the *definition* of cultural appropriation in our account, we agree that the existence of a power imbalance gives certain acts of cultural appropriation "a heightened normative importance" to which onlookers must pay attention.[9]

At least one significant complication emerges from directing attention toward the presence of power imbalances

Those who are privileged see their culture built into as well as reflected back by their local political and social institutions, and therefore do not need to actively protect and preserve valuable practices and symbols from misuse and disrespect by others.

that shape moments of cultural exchange between dominant and disadvantaged groups: How and when should we understand a disadvantaged group's decision or choice as authoritative under those conditions? Take, for example, the appropriation of cultural objects from disadvantaged groups. What is sometimes called the appropriation of cultural objects is frequently just plain theft; historically, "valuable objects, ranging from masks, carvings and manuscripts to pots and baskets have been looted by invaders, explorers, colonizers and governors." And yet some of these exchanges may have in fact been negotiated by representatives of cultural groups—in sociologist Andrea Walsh and philosopher Dominic McIver's analysis, the focus is on Indigenous communities, but the same is true in any colonial context—in ways that make it at least nominally unclear whether the exchanges were coerced or freely made. As Walsh and McIver observe in the case of Indigenous communities, "Many First Nations artifacts in Canadian collections came from communities that had long engaged in trading relationships with outsiders. By the legal standards of all parties, the purchase of some of these artifacts may sometimes have been legitimate."[10]

On the one hand, some may argue that the conditions of colonialism and the radical power imbalances that attend it are such that no exchanges made under those conditions can be treated as legitimate. Indigenous communities that suffered (and continue to suffer) under colonial institutions were dispossessed and without resources; their choices to exchange cultural artifacts for materials needed inside their communities were, effectively, forced. On the other hand, it is important to recognize that even under conditions of domination or oppression, disadvantaged groups can and do express agency, and with that in mind, it is crucial to avoid a paternalist orientation toward groups that have engaged in these exchanges by refusing to treat any of their choices under these conditions as manifesting their true preferences.

One way that power imbalances create the conditions under which wrongful cultural appropriation takes place is by enabling appropriators to *disregard* those from whom they are appropriating. Because of a power imbalance, appropriators may be unaware of or disinterested in the fact that the practices and symbols that are taken have deep, significant meaning to others, such that their appropriation is understood by those others as a lack of recognition or respect for them personally along with their cultures. This way of interpreting the wrong of cultural appropriation finds expression in Rebecca Tuvel's analysis; the wrong, she says, is *disregard*. She argues that those who appropriate express this disregard in the form of "(i.e., disrespect) or a kind of *looking away from* (i.e., indifference)." Tuvel considers an example that we also discussed in the introduction to the book, explaining that from her perspective (and we agree), when Cleveland's baseball team's fans appeared at games in American Indian regalia, they were not ignorant of the racist implications of their choices. Rather, they ignored them "because they simply do not care," and in their lack of care, they "actively show disregard for cultural others."[11]

A second way a power imbalance can create the conditions for wrongful cultural appropriation is in the form of perpetuating, among those in dominant communities, an ignorance of the history or meaning of the symbols or practices they are appropriating. Consider the choice of non-Black women to wear cornrows, which we touched on briefly in chapter 3, and that became a matter of public discussion when media personality Kylie Jenner circulated pictures of herself on social media wearing them. Or the choice of fashion designer Marc Jacobs, whose 2017 collection featured white models with dreadlocks. Why did Black people, and Black women in particular, express frustration with these choices? There is a long history of racial politics connected to Black women's hair in the United States. For example, a recent survey of US women from across racial and ethnic groups found that Black women's hair is much more likely to be described as unprofessional, and that Black women believed they had to straighten their hair to be successful in job interviews. Nearly 20 percent of the Black women in the survey reported having been sent home from work because of their hair, and nearly a quarter believed that their hair was the reason they were denied a job.[12] In conditions where Black women are penalized for their hair, it is angering to see a white woman *take* a traditional Black hairstyle and circulate images of herself like that for celebration in public spaces, without seeing or acknowledging that this same freedom is not as available to the Black women from whom this style originates.[13]

Neither Jenner nor Jacobs acted maliciously. Yet their actions demonstrate a lack of understanding that Black Americans have been penalized for wearing cornrows. When Jacobs tweeted in response to criticism, he showcased just how little he understood of his choices and their impacts: "All who cry 'cultural appropriation' or whatever nonsense about any race or skin colour wearing their hair in any particular style or manner—funny how you don't criticise women of colour for straightening their hair. . . . I am inspired by people and how they look, and don't see colour or race."[14] This specific wrong is rooted in the history and presence of systemic racism in the United States, which operates in ways that continue to treat Black Americans as second-class citizens. The wrong here is not quite that Jacobs's models wore dreadlocks; it is that Jacobs produced these fashions from within a system of injustice that allows him, but not those who originated the style, to benefit from it. And then, faced with criticism of his choices, Jacobs doubled down rather than acknowledge the imbalance his models manifested, as they walked down the runway wearing luxury clothing.

Jenner's wrong is part of a larger trend in which non-Black artists integrate elements of Black culture into their looks, presentations, and products. Leslie Bow, a scholar of Asian American studies, observes that there is a kind of fetishism of Black culture that is enabled by the existence of ongoing power imbalances between white and Black Americans. Some people, she says, believe that in taking cultural practices and symbols connected to Black culture, they are offering a kind of "homage because it appears to honor Black style, . . . [but] in reality, Blackfishing [the term given to these actions] situates that style as a commodity. It has the effect of reducing a people with a specific history to a series of appropriable traits or objects."[15] Those who naturally possess these traits, however, continue to suffer disadvantage.

Acts of cultural appropriation not only demonstrate marginalization and contribute to its persistence but can also *worsen* marginalization. Acts of appropriation in the context of power imbalances are accepted in the first place because those who are engaging in them are typically inattentive to or disinterested in the impact of their actions. This disinterest is a signal that those from whom the practices or symbols are taken are ignored in public spaces—the "group is treated as insignificant, unimportant, and unworthy of respect."[16] The act of appropriating worsens marginalization in at least two related ways: First, powerful groups take on a role that ought to belong to minority groups—that of signaling which practices and symbols are of importance—and second and correspondingly, powerful groups deny minority communities the opportunity to speak for themselves about what is important to their own culture. Minority groups are silenced or ignored—denied an opportunity to speak in public on their own behalf, their "voice" having been taken by those in comparatively more powerful positions. This denial can be understood, in our view, as a constraint on minority's freedom of expression; we will elaborate this claim further in chapter 6. The result is that powerful groups, by appropriating, shape how specific practices and symbols are understood by the majority—and typically, these depictions borrow from or generate cultural stereotypes and prejudices to which minority group members are then subject.[17]

Unjust Profit Making

The first amplifier, the existence of power imbalances—sustained by unjust institutions—makes it easier for appropriators to profit illegitimately from cultural appropriation, which is a second amplifier. In most of the cases we consider, the relevant profit is financial, though it need not be; profit could be in terms of other valuable resources, such as social status or power, reputation, and so on. Here we mean to highlight cases where appropriators *profit from* the cultural practices or symbols they have taken from disadvantaged communities, typically when they extract "excessive benefits" from "vulnerable individuals."[18] These actions exploit disadvantaged groups: "Exploitation occurs when cultural property is unfairly taken in a way that harms cultural members, while benefitting the appropriator," explains one scholar.[19] In this context, exploitation is characterized by the unfair taking of cultural property that benefits the taker, and often significantly.[20] There are two different wrongs here, which we consider below: One wrong is that a dominant group profits from practices it appropriates from marginalized groups in a context where those latter groups have experienced disadvantage when and by engaging in those practices themselves, and a second wrong is when a dominant group profits from the taking of minority practices and symbols when that minority ought rather to be the profiting group.

To be sure, not all acts of wrongful appropriation generate profit for the appropriators and not all forms of profit making are wrongful. When appropriators wear Indigenous headdresses to costume parties, they are engaging in appropriation—which is morally problematic—but there is no financial profit involved for the appropriator (although some social benefit might accrue to these appropriators). In some other cases, the appropriator is explicitly intending to gain financially, and that objective is not objectionable. Consider the example we raised in the introduction to this chapter: restauranteurs of one culture borrowing spices and flavors from another to prepare food. Here, while that may be a form of cultural appropriation and there is a profit motive, it does not seem to be wrongful in any significant way (though we will consider an instance below where it may be so).

The music industry presents additional illustrations of cultural exchange, only some of which may merit the label of wrongful cultural appropriation on the grounds of unjust profit making. To demonstrate, let us present and draw distinctions among three cases of musical exchange. Consider, first, Elvis Presley, who is sometimes described as having borrowed and profited from musical styles that were developed by, and central to, the African American musical scene. Presley wrote and performed music at a time when racism and discrimination against Black Americans was explicit as well as institutionally protected. When Presley borrowed from Black culture, he seemingly did so without attribution and without intending to benefit Black musicians, although his music did apparently introduce many white listeners to "Black" music—thereby inadvertently generating benefit for Black musicians. It is not that his appropriation of Black musical styles can be forgiven because of his social and political context, but given that context, it is possible to see that his choice generated some benefits to Black musicians even where the institutional context was one in which they were systematically disadvantaged.

Compare Presley to Eminem, another white musician whose musical style is clearly influenced by Black musical styles and who has profited as a result. He has been explicitly accused of cultural appropriation. Eminem, however, has been clear and vocal about the benefits he has enjoyed—compared to Black artists—because he is white.[21] One of the lyrics to "White America" is "let's do the math: if I was Black, I would've sold half." He has in general successfully defended himself from accusations of cultural appropriation via his ongoing collaborations with and evident respect for Black musicians. Furthermore, he has demonstrated a commitment to elevating their voices across multiple contexts.[22] For example, he publicly used his platform to defend the right of Black athletes to "take a knee" in objection to police violence against Black Americans.[23] The upshot here is that, as we will elaborate in the final chapter, acts of apparent cultural appropriation can be rendered nonappropriative under some conditions. So, while at first glance Eminem's actions may appear appropriative, a closer examination suggests his way of proceeding may not in fact be problematically appropriative. We return to cases like this one, where certain ways of proceeding—as we will describe, by respecting the principles of equitable engagement and respectful collaboration—may be such as to render otherwise culturally appropriative acts nonappropriative.[24]

Finally, compare Presley and Eminem to Iggy Azalea, another white rapper, but one who is widely accused of cultural appropriation for the ways in which she appears to be presenting herself *as* Black and attempting to gain profit by taking on the features of a Black racial identity. She has been accused, for example, of adopting a "blaccent" (she allegedly responded to this claim by explaining that it felt weird to rap with her own Australian accent) and making her skin appear to be darker than it is.[25] According to her critics, her "product" is the presentation of herself as racially ambiguous rather than as the white Australian she is. What distinguishes Azalea from Eminem is her attempt to portray herself as Black (or at least of ambiguous race) along with her lack of attention to the ways in which Black artists can be and have been penalized for the racial identity she is attempting to capitalize on. So while Presley, Eminem, and Azalea all profit from engaging with "Black" music, only Azalea appears open to criticism that she is engaging in harmful cultural appropriation—made harmful by her attempt to profit from taking on traits typically connected to Black artists, without any attention directed to or awareness of the challenges that Black artists have faced in capitalizing on these very same traits. The purpose of this brief comparison is to respond to the observation that music, like food, seems to be a space where "appropriation" ought at least sometimes to be welcomed rather than criticized—and also to notice that there are cases where although we believe it should be permitted and encouraged (as in the music industry), some forms of it remain objectionable.

One space where the profit motive of appropriation is in clear evidence, in ways that are more frequently problematic, is in the fashion industry. Recall here the objections, which we considered earlier, that the Sikh community raised against the use of turbans. For instance, upscale fashion brand Balenciaga generated controversy when it marketed a pair of sweatpants—the "trompe l'oeil" pants—that were accused of appropriating from Black culture. The offending pants in that case featured material that made it appear as though red and green boxer shorts were visible from the top of the otherwise gray sweatpants—a style that has traditionally been connected to hip-hop culture and is often said to have originated in prisons, where convicts were not permitted to wear belts with their pants.[26] Critics of Balenciaga's pants accused it of appropriating a product from Black culture, which Black citizens have historically been penalized for wearing, and profiting from it.

Over the course of the early 2000s, many US local governments and school systems passed laws banning so-called saggy pants.[27] For example, one local government in Louisiana passed an "indecent exposure" regulation, which prohibited wearing pants that intentionally showed the wearer's underwear.[28] In defending the law, the then mayor explained specifically that the government was not intending to target Black men and boys, saying, "White people wear sagging pants, too." But as an NPR reporter notes, "This drama around young brown kids, baggy clothes and crime goes back much further than hip-hop."[29] In 2020, when the municipal government in Opa-locka, Florida, repealed its "saggy pants ordinances," it did so by observing the disproportionate impact on "certain segments of our population, including Black and brown men and women."[30] It is important to see this history of penalizing streetwear most often worn by Black men and boys, and of taking that form of streetwear as evidence of disrespect and likely criminality, when interpreting the response to Balenciaga's fashion line.

In chapter 3, we considered the Sikh response to the wearing of turbans by fashion models. We suggested the wrong was located in the choice to market—as a fashion accessory—a deeply held spiritual practice and symbol. Sikhs objected not specifically to the profit that was set to be made from selling a "gorgeous" turban, although they did object to that as well, but instead to the commercialization of a spiritual practice. There, just as in the case of Balenciaga, the wrong is not quite that profit was made by a dominant group at the expense of a disadvantaged group.

Rather, what renders these two cases problematic, and the second perhaps more so than the first, is the presence of unjust circumstances that render a particular practice dangerous to engage in for one culture but profit worthy for another. From the perspective of those who witness their cultural practices being appropriated by profit-making entities—baggy pants and turban wearing—it feels unfair, in the sense of being a double standard, that others can engage in these practices without experiencing mistreatment or harassment. In these cases, the wrong is not that Sikhs or Black Americans might have profited instead had these fashion moguls refrained from appropriating; they are not *stealing* profits that might otherwise have flowed to disadvantaged community members, in other words. What is wrong is that only one group, the group in a position of privilege, can profit from these practices at all, while those from whom these practices are appropriated experience penalties for doing the same. To return to the earlier discussion of structural injustice, in this instance, not only are appropriators at fault for taking advantage of unjust circumstances that permit them to profit from a symbol or practice, even if the cultural originators cannot or do not, but they are also in part responsible for creating and sustaining the conditions of structural injustice that we described in relation to the sustaining of unjust power imbalances, and thus share responsibility for dismantling them. So the wrongdoer is the appropriator and also the sustainer of (or someone who refuses to participate in the undermining of) unjust institutions.

A separate wrong is committed where appropriators make profits from a practice or symbol that, had it been left in the hands of the community from which it emerged, would have enabled that community to benefit from it. One scholar describes this situation as a form of exploitation where "cultural property is unfairly taken in a way that harms cultural members, while benefitting the appropriator."[31] In chapter 5, we consider in some more detail cases where non-Indigenous people make profit from mimicking Indigenous art styles and by leading customers to believe their products are authentically Indigenous.

For now, let us return to an example we considered briefly in the introduction to the book and earlier in this chapter, and that may seem trivial: the choice of one group to prepare and market food that is traditionally associated with another one. One of the great benefits of migration is that ways of preparing food travel across borders, allowing so many of us to benefit from new and often better tastes. One of the authors grew up in a small Canadian city and recalls with great fondness when the first Chinese restaurant opened up in town, offering respite from the endless pizza chains! No one, it seems, should be understood to "own" flavors or spices, or ways of preparing foods, in ways that exclude others from using or enjoying them. Yet Jamie Oliver's choice to market a form of "jerk rice" nevertheless raised alarm bells among those who oppose cultural appropriation.

Here is what happened: Oliver created a product that he labeled "punch jerk rice." Critics objected to the ingredient list. Few of the items listed there feature in a traditional Jamaican jerk marinade, which, they said, is typically used on chicken: "Jerk rice isn't really a thing."[32] A Labour member of Parliament waded into the debate, tweeting, "Your jerk rice is not OK. This appropriation from Jamaica needs to stop."[33] Oliver defended his choice, maintaining that as a chef, he experiments with "flavours and spices from all over the world . . . learning and drawing inspiration from different countries and cultures."[34] Our view is that this defense is a reasonable one. But it does not capture what people were angry about, which, as British newspaper columnist Zoe Williams wrote, "isn't the homely cross-pollination of one tasty thing with another, but that a person who is already minted is making a load of money out of a bastardised version of something, while the people who eat the authentic dish make diddly-squat from it."[35] The objection, in other words, concerns the way in which unjust structures of inequality allow for Oliver to make money selling something called "jerk" when those who have developed jerk in the first place are not able to do the same. It is an objection that Oliver's profit is in part *at the expense of* comparatively poorer Jamaican immigrants to the United Kingdom. According to this analysis, would-be Jamaican chefs face a "loss of economic potential" because of Oliver's choices.[36] Perhaps, as some people say, some customers will choose to purchase Oliver's jerk product rather than jerk products produced by Jamaican chefs, maybe because they recognize his name and are comfortable with his brand. Perhaps, though, the result of consuming Oliver's jerk rice is that those who have done so are misled about "real" Jamaican flavors and therefore are less open-minded about frequenting Jamaican restaurants on the grounds that the jerk-flavored food served there is not what they are expecting. (Whether such is, in fact, the case requires additional investigation.)

In the final chapter, we consider in some detail how to proceed if cultural appropriation is to be avoided. One proposal we will consider there is whether, in cases where profits are unjustly acquired by appropriators, it is a reasonable response for those appropriators to return some or even all of the profit to the relevant disadvantaged community. When French designer Chanel decided to make and sell boomerangs, for example, a symbol deeply connected to Australian Indigenous communities, one critic responded that "I sincerely hope that @CHANEL is donating all the profits to underprivileged aboriginal communities."[37]

Evaluating Cultural Appropriation Claims

In chapter 1, we acknowledged the difficulties of distinguishing acts of cultural appropriation from those of cultural engagement. Many critics of the concept of cultural appropriation argue that "taking" symbols and practices from other cultures should be understood as a form of a compliment, and that human history just *is* the exchange of ideas and goods among cultures. Consistent with those who express skepticism of cultural appropriation claims, we agree that there are cases where the wrong that is generated appears minimal or insignificant.

In chapter 2, we described that our objective is to offer a normative account of cultural appropriation that treats all acts of taking as presumptively wrong. But we also aim to take account of Matthes's intuition that some acts are more wrong than others. Our objective in this chapter has been to identify two distinct features that, when present, render an act of appropriation especially wrongful. Crucially, in our view, these amplifiers do not define a wrong but rather make an act that is presumptively wrong even worse. Correspondingly, assessing claims of wrongful cultural appropriation necessarily requires evaluating whether one or both of these amplifiers are present.

We might therefore understand acts of cultural appropriation—and the extent to which any one is wrong—on a kind of continuum, where those that take place in the presence of none of the amplifiers are trivial and those that take place in the presence of both of them are significantly wrong. Most acts of cultural appropriation are somewhere on the continuum between these extremes.

Placing an act along this continuum does not automatically mean, from our perspective, that appropriators are morally bound to stop what they are doing. The question of whether appropriators ought to cease their actions, and the issue of whether social or state sanction is warranted, is something we consider in the final chapter of the book. For now, we are simply observing that there are cases of cultural appropriation in which both of the amplifiers are present, and hence where the claims of moral wrongness are legitimate and should be taken seriously. The final chapter considers where and when these claims are strong enough that they merit intervention, what sort of intervention is available to respond to them, and whether and when there are competing considerations such that intervention might not be called for, even where a significant moral wrong has taken place. Before we do that, we turn next to the paradigmatic case of appropriation: from Indigenous Peoples.

5

CULTURAL APPROPRIATION, CULTURAL GENOCIDE, AND INDIGENOUS PEOPLES

In the previous chapter, we described two amplifiers that, as we explained, are generally what turn merely trivial acts of cultural appropriation into wrongful ones. In this chapter, we examine the appropriation of acts and practices that are central to Indigenous Peoples specifically, beyond the deployment of Indigenous symbols and practices in sports, which we discussed in the introduction. Recall the amplifiers that increase the wrongfulness of cultural appropriation: the existence of a power imbalance between the agent who is appropriating and the culture from which they are appropriating, and the presence of profit making by the appropriator, often at the expense of (or sometimes with disregard for) the cultural group from which the symbol or practice was appropriated. The presence of either of these amplifiers makes an act of cultural appropriation wrongful, and the presence of both signals the worst forms of cultural appropriation. As we will demonstrate, such is the case of most appropriation of Indigenous culture by non-Indigenous peoples in the context of settler colonialism. More specifically, we identify the cultural appropriation of Indigenous practices and symbols as one crucial element of the ongoing cultural genocide that was and still is a key part of the settler colonial project. The consequences of long-term settler colonialism and especially its (failed but damaging) attempts at cultural genocide, both of which we will define shortly, are such that both amplifiers are generally present in the context of appropriation from Indigenous Peoples.

In this chapter, we begin with a brief account of the persistence of settler colonialism along with the harms it continues to inflict on Indigenous Peoples to make the uncontroversial case that in spite of decades of Indigenous activism and recent attention to the difficulties that Indigenous Peoples face, Indigenous Peoples largely remain oppressed across settler colonial states. The harms of settler colonialism and the attendant cultural genocide persist and, as we discuss below, have a significant impact on how acts of appropriation should be interpreted. Second, we examine briefly the forms of offense and misrepresentation as well as the consequent misrecognition that Indigenous Peoples face so that they can be distinguished from acts of appropriation, and so we can identify the connections among them. Third, we outline four distinct forms

The cultural appropriation of Indigenous practices and symbols is one crucial element of the ongoing cultural genocide that was and still is a key part of the settler colonial project.

of appropriation to which Indigenous Peoples are subject, all of which are wrongful. These are the appropriation of artifacts, spiritual and artistic practices, and identities. Of these, the last warrants special assessment, and we devote some time to looking at the recent attempts to uncover non-Indigenous peoples, so-called pretendians or race shifters, who, for a wide range of reasons, have appropriated Indigenous identities for personal gain.

Settler Colonialism

Historically, settler colonialism has been defined by the movement to colonies of large numbers of European citizens who, in settling, displaced and dispossessed the original, Indigenous inhabitants.[1] Settler colonialism, the form of colonialism that characterizes Canada, Scandinavia, Australia, and the United States, differs from the (largely) extractive colonialism that marked the colonizing of African states—in which European colonizers operated with the intent mainly of extracting the material resources present on African territory (including its people) and benefiting from them. The consequences of settler colonialism are well documented: Indigenous populations were decimated by the diseases that traveled with European colonizers, then by violence directed at them, and then by the systematic theft of land on which Indigenous

Peoples relied to support themselves and their ways of life.[2] As Yann Allard-Tremblay and Elaine Coburn explain, the objective of settler colonialism was "the elimination of the native, either through assimilation, displacement, or extermination." It is not complete, they continue, until Indigenous Peoples have been eradicated, and no longer threaten "settler occupation and sovereignty."[3]

One key tool of settler colonialism has since been labeled "cultural genocide," referring to a concerted effort to destroy Indigenous cultures. As a practice, cultural genocide does not focus on killing members of cultural minorities but rather aims to destroy the foundations of their culture, including its languages, practices, and traditions, so that it is no longer viable.[4] The attack on Indigenous culture historically came in many forms. For example, across settler states, Indigenous children were forcibly removed from their families and placed in residential schools. The explicit goal of these schools was to "civilize" Indigenous children; the logic was that by removing Indigenous children from their families, families would thereby be prevented from passing on Indigenous cultural and spiritual practices to their children, and by forcing children to speak English (or French) rather than their own languages and to participate in Christian (as opposed to Indigenous) spiritual practices, the "Indian" in them could be erased. As well, settler colonial states practiced forms of forced sterilization of Indigenous women and effectively stole children from Indigenous families (citing dangers to "child welfare") to be raised in white families as white. These practices and many others contributed to the weakening and destruction of Indigenous cultures.

The specific form of cultural genocide that is relevant to our analysis is the wide-ranging set of laws that denied Indigenous Peoples the right to practice their culture or religion. In the United States, the ban on such practices was in place until the passage of the 1978 American Indian Religious Freedom Act.[5] Similarly, the 1876 Indian Act, which in a modified form continues to govern elements of the relationship between the Canadian government and Indigenous Peoples, originally made many kinds of public expressions of Indigeneity illegal. The practice of Indigenous religion was made illegal, and Indigenous Peoples were not permitted to appear in public shows or performances wearing their ceremonial dress.[6] Most cultural ceremonies were also made illegal, including in particular the potlatch, "a gift-giving feast that was traditionally used to mark a variety of important milestones and occasions in West Coast tribes and customs, and as a way of celebrating life." Although the laws banning these practices were ultimately reversed, the reversal transpired only after many generations of Indigenous Peoples had been denied the opportunity to grow up and live in thriving cultures that could impart to them pride as well as confidence in the value of their own cultural and spiritual practices.[7] The importance of a robust culture in producing and protecting the conditions under which individuals can live flourishing lives has been well established elsewhere.[8] Contemporary Indigenous resurgence is at least in part about revitalizing these practices *internal* to Indigenous communities so that their cultures can thrive again.[9]

The remedies for extractive colonialism have typically involved the departure of colonizers from (mainly) African land and the consequent returning of political authority to the original inhabitants alongside at least some financial compensation for the goods extracted from those lands. The remedies for settler colonialism are less clear—since settlers and their descendants (as well as more recent immigrants) remain on Indigenous land, from which they cannot easily depart, new, noncolonial ways of engaging with each other are required.[10] Evidence that the harms of settler colonialism persist and that Indigenous Peoples remain oppressed is abundant: Indigenous Peoples remain undereducated compared to the wider population; they often live in underresourced territory, where clean water and quality health care are difficult to access; and they are overrepresented among those who are incarcerated and among those who take up shelter spaces in urban areas.[11] Across settler colonial states, there is growing awareness that extraordinary wrongs were perpetrated against Indigenous Peoples and that these wrongs persist, and the need for some form of remedy is increasingly widely recognized. Efforts at reconciliation have made at least some progress in addressing the wrongs of colonialism, and in the concluding chapter we will consider the ways in which taking active steps to avoid appropriating the cultural artifacts, acts, practices, and identities of Indigenous Peoples can be a part of them.

One major victory in the global project to recognize Indigenous Peoples and their rights was the development of the United Nations Declaration on the Rights of Indigenous Peoples (UNDRIP), a resolution adopted by the UN General Assembly in 2007 with 143 signatories. Initially the major settler states—Australia, New Zealand, Canada, and the United States—voted against UNDRIP, but they have all since endorsed it. UNDRIP highlights the specific cultural rights that Indigenous Peoples have to control their own cultural expression as well as the products that derive from their cultural and spiritual traditions. For example, Article 11 reads in part,

> Indigenous Peoples have the right to practise and revitalize their cultural traditions and customs. This includes the right to maintain, protect and develop the past, present and future manifestations of their cultures, such as archaeological and historical sites, artefacts, designs, ceremonies, technologies and visual and performing arts and literature.

And Article 31 reads,

> Indigenous Peoples have the right to maintain, control, protect and develop their cultural heritage, traditional knowledge and traditional cultural expressions, as well as the manifestations of their sciences, technologies and cultures, including human and genetic resources, seeds, medicines, knowledge of the properties of fauna and flora, oral traditions, literatures, designs, sports and traditional games and visual and performing arts. They also have the right to maintain, control, protect and develop their intellectual property over such cultural heritage, traditional knowledge, and traditional cultural expressions.[12]

The importance of moving forward in ways that respect the rights of Indigenous Peoples, including in relation to their culture and spirituality, shapes our discussion of the special wrongfulness of the cultural appropriation of Indigenous artifacts, spiritual and artistic practices, and identities.

Offense and Misrepresentation

Recall from chapter 3 that a cultural offense is an offense that hurts others by attacking their cultural beliefs and practices, that cultural misrepresentation is the giving of a false or misleading account of a culture's practices or beliefs, and that they both generate and perpetuate a form of cultural misrecognition that demonstrates a willful disregard or disrespect for those practices and beliefs.[13] Although this chapter focuses mainly on appropriative actions taken against Indigenous Peoples, let us note first that Indigenous Peoples are no strangers to cultural offense and misrepresentation. Offense can be minor or more significant. For instance, some recent research suggests that there has been a rise in the number of Canadians who deny the negative impact of residential schools on Indigenous Peoples, rejecting the claim that they were harmful (rather than educative) and questioning, say, the truth of recent discoveries of unmarked graves at the sites of these schools.[14] A recent report details denialists entering one such site at night with shovels, allegedly intending to assess for themselves the truth of the claim that remains of children's bodies had been found.[15] The visitors were "disrespectful of the site, breaching cultural protocols and taking videos and pictures of the burial area without permission"—in what is a clear instance of profound cultural offense.[16] Denialists often argue, against extensive evidence to the contrary, that Canada adopted a benevolent and generous stance toward Indigenous Peoples, and therefore that they ought to be grateful to the Canadian state for what it has provided them.

As well, stereotypes, the most common form of misrepresentation, of Indigenous Peoples abound. Historically many of the stereotypes of Indigenous Peoples presented them as barbaric and uncivilized, and often casually violent, requiring taming by civilized Europeans. More recent stereotypes have tended to focus on the struggles Indigenous Peoples face after decades of colonialist oppression, frequently decontextualizing the source of the struggles and instead presenting them as somehow inherent to Indigenous culture.[17] Misrepresentation of Indigenous cultural practices and symbols abounds too, as demonstrated, for example, by the casual construction and display of dreamcatchers at summer camps, without attention to the spiritual meaning that attends them.[18]

Offense toward and misrepresentation of Indigenous Peoples often travel with cultural appropriation.

Cultural Appropriation of Indigeneity

Consider a first form of cultural appropriation: the appropriation of Indigenous cultural artifacts for display in museums. Note that the appropriation here is not in the theft of objects specifically; as we explained earlier, in our view, theft of cultural objects is just theft. To repeat our example from chapter 2, a person visiting the Taj Mahal who steals a statue is engaging in theft, even though the theft is of a cultural object. What renders the theft culturally appropriative is the subsequent display of these objects, alongside the thief's telling of the stories of those objects, including how they were stolen and what their meaning is or was to the culture to which they rightfully belong. There are hundreds if not thousands of Indigenous artifacts displayed in museums around the world, and recently there has been a general acceptance that these have largely been stolen or extracted under duress—"thousands of Indigenous artifacts have been confiscated or coerced from Indigenous communities, and many more objects were stolen from graves and sacred sites"—and that the return of these objects is fair and appropriate.[19] As we outlined earlier, UNDRIP has called on countries with a colonial past to respect the rights of Indigenous Peoples to their culture, and in part this requires that such countries think seriously about how to remedy the wrong of stolen property from Indigenous Peoples and its misrepresentation in public spaces.[20] In Canada, and consistent with UNDRIP, one major recommendation made by the 2015 Truth and Reconciliation Commission—a commission that gave public space to Indigenous Peoples to explain the impact of Canada's residential school system, and that released a report alongside ninety-four "calls to action" to facilitate reconciliation—was with respect to the urgency of protecting Indigenous traditional, cultural knowledge.[21]

In some cases, this objective could be accomplished through the return of traditional artifacts to the Indigenous community that produced them. A challenge that Indigenous advocates face in accomplishing the return of stolen cultural objects is the perception among museum curators that they are better placed than Indigenous Peoples to preserve them.[22] Yet prompted by the commission recommendations and UNDRIP, museums in Canada and around the world are increasingly willing to collaborate to secure the return of cultural and religious artifacts to Indigenous communities. For example, after three years of negotiation, a Manchester museum agreed to return nearly two hundred items, effectively stolen and shipped to Britain in 1771, belonging to the Anindilyakwa community in Australia. The curator of the museum, Georgina Young, described the motivation for negotiating the return of the items in terms of respecting UNDRIP recommendations, saying, "We are excited by all that this return makes possible in terms of . . . how it supports Anindilyakwa cultural strengthening for years to come."[23]

Controversy over a collection of Indigenous artifacts in Germany, however, highlights that the commitment to returning artifacts is not yet a matter of consensus. The Karl May Museum in Radebeul, Germany, celebrates German writer Karl May, who wrote popular novels set in the US West, published in the late nineteenth and early twentieth centuries. The novels feature a protagonist, Old

Shatterhand, and his companion, "Winnetou," "wise chief of the Apache Tribe," traveling through the US West to fight various injustices. After the author's death, his wife set about celebrating his legacy by establishing the museum, in part with Indigenous cultural objects she purchased from another non-Indigenous collector. Among the most controversial of these items were actual human scalps, the provenance of which was unclear; after some initial resistance, the curator of the museum agreed that the *display* of human remains as museum pieces is problematic and agreed to remove them. Until 2021, though, the museum refused to return any of the scalps, citing ambiguity about their origin (not all are believed to be Indigenous) and therefore also about to whom they should be returned. A researcher for the museum said, "The question is, who has the right to claim things back? That's the crucial question here."[24] In 2021, the museum agreed to repatriate one scalp to the Chippewa Nation, but said in doing so, "No evidence of any wrongdoing or colonial origin has been confirmed."[25] In spite of this insistence, the return of this scalp is a success—in part because a presumed-Indigenous body part was returned to its people, and in part because a symbol of a practice considered murderously barbaric is no longer on public display.

A second source of controversy and frustration stems from the museum's presentation of Indigenous Peoples more generally, as a historical people, with cultures that are "frozen in time" at the point of their alleged death, rather than as living and vibrant peoples who have survived decades of settler colonialism. In a scathing assessment of the museum's collection and its manner of presenting the items (often factually incorrectly), scholar Lisa Michelle King writes that the museum "perpetuates inaccurate and potentially harmful stereotypes of Native American peoples that serve German and European audiences at the expense of Native communities and nations."[26] Relating her experience of another display adopting the same orientation toward the presentation of Indigenous Peoples, Tawnya Plain Eagle tells the story of visiting a museum in Calgary, Canada, and observing an exhibit of her own community, the Blackfoot. Her interpretation of the motivation to keep Indigenous artifacts on display is "to advance the idea that we are people of the past. It's part of a Western narrative that tries to erase the true history of what happened to Indigenous people on this continent."[27]

The artifacts on display across museums have, as we explained in chapter 3 and again just above, largely been stolen from Indigenous communities. The theft of cultural items was common across colonized states as well as in war more generally, and is increasingly recognized as wrong. What is distinct in the case of the theft of Indigenous cultural items is that it often occurred at the same time as (or just prior to) a legal regime that banned Indigenous cultural practices and the production of cultural artifacts connected to them. Settlers from multiple walks of life therefore had a convenient justification for "confiscating" these illegalized items, which then found their way into museums and private collections around the world. The explanation for the legitimacy of this theft was in part described in terms of preserving the "final remnants of a dying race."[28] This fiction, that Indigenous Peoples were dying and thereby required remembering through the display of their artifacts, persists in many of the narratives that accompany the display of Indigenous artifacts—as in the exhibits at the Karl May Museum. (In chapter 6, we will consider nonappropriative ways for museums to engage with material stolen from Indigenous communities as well as other disadvantaged communities.)

The appropriation of Indigenous cultural and spiritual *practices* is a second form of harmful cultural appropriation. For example, the so-called wellness industry—the set of firms that offer consumers products and instructions aimed at adopting a healthy way of life—is at fault here for borrowing and modifying Indigenous practices to sell to Western customers who may not be aware of (or care about) their origins. The industry, for instance, has recently been criticized for marketing the practice of "saging" (the burning of sage), which, among others, actress Gwyneth Paltrow's company Goop had promoted to clear "bad vibes" (after much criticism, Goop no longer offers saging kits). Saging borrows from the sacred Indigenous practice of smudging, the ritual of "burning of plants in order to cleanse one's space, initiate prayer, or bring about peaceful energy," which is observed across many Indigenous cultures.[29] One Indigenous activist observes, "Smudging sage has nothing to do with the magical room-cleansing nonsense sold by uninspired capitalists"; speaking of her own Lakota culture, rather "sage is a critical component within Lakota medicinal and ceremonial knowledge."[30] Similarly, Western interest in Indigenous sweat lodge ceremonies has increased, with them being marketed as a kind of spa treatment in which participants can "detoxify" their body as opposed to being understood as a deeply held spiritual practice at the center of many Indigenous communities. As one Indigenous practitioner notes of sweat lodge ceremonies, "When and why it is held, how we dress, how we enter . . . what prayer songs we sing. . . . It is an ancient ritual that has been practiced virtually the same for thousands of years." It is, she says, a "religious ceremony," and referring to it otherwise, or offering it as one of a menu of "wellness options," is "an insult."[31]

The proliferation of commercial ayahuasca retreats in the Amazon has been subject to the same criticism.[32] Over the last fifteen years, these retreats have become increasingly popular as Western tourists travel to the Amazon—specifically to the Peruvian city of Iquitos, which is the center of this form of tourism—to consume ayahuasca, a psychedelic drink made from a variety of plants that "has long been part of the deep-rooted spiritual traditions of Indigenous Amazonian societies that use it in a specific ritualized way," often under the "supervision" of a "shaman."[33] Ayahuasca's central active ingredient is illegal in most countries; Indigenous Peoples have an exception on religious grounds in the United States, permitting them to use it as part of traditional ceremonies. As a result, non-Indigenous peoples who are keen to consume it legally must fly to South America to do so.

The physical experience of consuming ayahuasca is uncomfortable; many people feel sick to their stomachs and vomit or clear their bowels, and many sweat and get agitated as well as dizzy. These experiences of "purging" are described by those who offer the drink as key to receiving the relevant benefits. Moreover, explains one writer, people may "witness varied hallucinations. . . . [T]hey may also get a sense of being visited or inhabited by an alien consciousness." At least from an Indigenous perspective, however, what matters is not so much the experiences themselves but instead how they are interpreted. These interpretations ought to be carried out by trained Indigenous Peoples to ensure that they are "grounded in distinct local beliefs and cultural systems."[34]

A positive reading of this trend is that Western interest in ayahuasca can generate economic benefit for many Indigenous communities living in and around the Amazon, which, like Indigenous communities globally, suffer from high rates of poverty.[35] The benefits might come from increased tourism to the area in general and the opportunities for local Indigenous people to find jobs that emerge from increased tourism.

Yet as critics point out, those who run these centers are often non-Indigenous and thus the economic benefits do not necessarily flow to the Indigenous Peoples whose cultural practices are being shared with tourists. One activist observes that ayahuasca tourism is "making some people very rich, yet the [I]ndigenous communities where these practices originated continue to live in poverty." An Indigenous tourist operator, catering to tourists to Peru, refuses to offer this form of experimentation as an option, even though Westerners are clearly interested in it, saying, "We don't offer those kinds of trips because we do respect our people, the costumes, [and] traditions," and that the rituals connected to these cultures "need to be understood and respected" rather than exploited for profit.[36] One might say, well, if this tour operator does not offer ayahuasca experiences for spiritual reasons, they are not harmed economically by those who do; it is at least in principle possible that this is true.[37] Yet since Westerners are seeking ayahuasca experiences specifically, the result for this Indigenous tour operator and others like them is less profit overall. Many operators will offer multiple tours and services, and so where tourists arrive seeking specifically one experience and are open to others, those operators who do not offer the sought-after experience will suffer economically.

One distinct harm to Indigenous communities in the Amazon from the presence of popular ayahuasca retreats appears to be in the distortion of their internal cultural practices. For example, in some cases, Indigenous communities whose culture did not include ayahuasca use have adopted it as a tradition at least in part to cater to Westerners.[38] Although some describe this behavior as "native appropriation," it is hard to fault marginalized communities themselves for attempting to profit from Western interest. One writer documents that street kids in Iquitos tell her that they want to be "shamans" when they grow up to take advantage of the profits available to be made from Western tourists—money that is made from selling the "kids' own cultural traditions while they suffer from high levels of poverty."[39] Additionally, for those communities that do practice ayahuasca consumption, the cost of ayahuasca has risen significantly because of the increased tourist demand, and as a result, some Indigenous Peoples find that "access to their own healing traditions, a cornerstone of their cultural heritage," is closed.[40] The danger of this "interest" in profiting from cultural practices affects Western tourists as well. One consequence, for instance, of the inflow of tourists is an increase in self-styled experts without significant (or any) experience in or connection to the consumption of ayahuasca who offer to guide foreigners in its use. Increasingly there are reports of abuse, physical and sexual, as well as forms of negligence "at the hands of predatory and inept shamans," all of which put tourists' lives at risk; although it is rare, several deaths have been reported at the hands of untrained "shamans."[41]

These first two forms of cultural appropriation—of artifacts and practices—share several features in common: The artifacts and practices are "taken" from Indigenous Peoples without their consent, non-Indigenous peoples are shaping the way in which Indigenous culture is understood more widely (and in some cases, how it is practiced too), and non-Indigenous peoples profit from what they have taken from Indigenous Peoples, and at their expense. The next two types of appropriation are slightly different in form: the appropriation of traditionally Indigenous artistic practices, which raises questions about fair ways to engage in cultural exchange, and the appropriation of Indigenous identities, which raises questions about benefits that are reserved for Indigenous Peoples as part of settler states' attempts at reconciliation, but that are allotted to non-Indigenous individuals.

A third form of appropriation is of distinctive Indigenous artistic forms or practices, including traditionally Indigenous ways of painting, sculpting, dancing, and creating music, including their for-profit sales. A 2010 study carried out in the city of Vancouver estimated that of the

"Indigenous-themed" souvenirs available in gifts shops around the city, nearly 90 percent were produced and sold without any connection to Indigenous artists themselves.[42] The report documents the deliberate attempt to mislead customers into thinking the products have Indigenous connection, such as by referring to art created by "Native Canadians," confusing the distinction between Indigenous Peoples and the much larger group of Canadians born on Canadian territory, or as "Painted on an Indian Reserve," without specifying that the painter was not Indigenous.[43] Australia faces the same difficulty, with recent research suggesting that up to 80 percent of the products marketed as Indigenous in gift shops were inauthentic—either made by non-Indigenous artists or mass-produced abroad.[44]

The creation and selling of inauthentic Indigenous art demonstrates that there is a real appetite for these products—just as the commercialization of ayahuasca retreats shows. Yet so long as this practice persists, Indigenous artisans are disadvantaged when attempting to offer their own products for sale for at least two reasons: first, because the individual work that goes into each piece of art is more significant than the work that goes into the mass-produced Indigenous-appearing products that compete with them in stores, thereby rendering the genuine products more expensive and less competitive, and second, because they do not have an easy way to access mass-market sales.[45] One nongovernmental organization that focuses on generating awareness of the importance of purchasing Indigenous art directly from Indigenous artists observes that "we see a direct link between the importation of internationally made 'Indigenous' items, such as dream-catchers, masks, totems, statues, moccasins, images and other objects, and the devaluation of authentic, Indigenous art."[46] The result is that many Indigenous artists struggle to make a living from their own art.

Whereas the deliberate attempt to mislead customers who may be keen to purchase authentic Indigenous art is fraudulent and evidently wrong, another form of artistic engagement is more complicated to assess. Given the beauty and originality of Indigenous forms of artistry, it is not surprising that non-Indigenous peoples have long been inspired by Indigenous artistic practices and have emulated them in their own creations. To take just one example, white artist Amanda PL spent several years at Lakehead University in Thunder Bay, Canada, where she learned and adopted a painting style titled "Woodlands" that is traditional to the Anishinaabe people. PL did not claim she was Indigenous. At Lakehead University, she learned the "untold history of Canada" with an Anishinaabe teacher, and notes that she has spent years "learning about aboriginal history, stories and teachings to promote integration and reconciliation among different Canadian cultures by bringing them together in celebration of peace and unity."[47]

In 2017, she was set to have a first exhibit when at the request of Indigenous activists, the hosting gallery called it off. In explaining its choice to cancel the show, the gallery's operators stated that on reflection with Indigenous activists, they came to believe it was not appropriate to give a non-Indigenous artist a platform to display her Indigenous-inspired art when Indigenous artists do not have that same platform.[48] In applauding the gallery's decision, one Indigenous artist observed that while the art produced by PL may have been beautiful, her art was created without the appropriate connection to the stories and tradition behind it—and these connections and stories are integral to the art itself.[49] In this case, PL was criticized for adopting artistic practices allegedly divorced from the tradition from which they emerged. In response, PL said that she did not set out to "steal" an art form or artistic practice to which she was not entitled; rather, it was just one of many styles she became acquainted and fell in love with over the course of her art education.

Another non-Indigenous artist faced a connected criticism. As in the case of PL, white artist Sue Coleman incorporated Indigenous artistic practices into her own Western-style paintings. Like PL, Coleman did not present herself as Indigenous, but she encountered considerable criticism when she described herself as a kind of translator of Indigenous artistic practices.[50] Her self-appointment as a translator was offensive, said Indigenous artist Carey

Newman, who wrote an open letter objecting to Coleman's self-portrayal that was signed by over a hundred people, many of them prominent Indigenous artists. He maintained, "We do not need you or anyone else to 'translate' our art form. . . . It is not only offensive and patronizing that you believe translation is needed, it is also disturbing that you have appointed yourself as the translator."[51]

In these instances, the appropriation is of an artistic practice, and whether this form of appropriation is objectionable is the subject of considerable dispute. Artists are well known to exchange techniques and styles, and generally this exchange is understood to be not only normal but valuable too. Yet as we articulated in chapter 3, these exchanges must take place on an equal playing field rather than under conditions in which one party to the exchange is in a position of dominance over the other.[52] In the case of exchanges between Indigenous and non-Indigenous artists, what makes them more appropriative, and wrongfully so, is in large part the background colonial infrastructure that persists in marginalizing Indigenous Peoples. This colonial infrastructure preserves a power imbalance between Indigenous and non-Indigenous peoples, such that the so-called exchange of artistic practices—from Indigenous to non-Indigenous artists—is nonconsensual as opposed to freely undertaken. Correspondingly, Indigenous Peoples may be less likely, in these circumstances, to profit from the art they have produced and the artistic practices they developed over time; instead, the attention and associated profit flows to non-Indigenous artists who have incorporated Indigenous practices into their art. This statement makes it seem like art is a zero-sum game: that if a non-Indigenous artist is offered space to show their (Indigenous-inspired) art, they are *replacing* an Indigenous artist who would otherwise have been offered the space. There is no direct evidence that such a trade-off is in place, such as with respect to PL's planned and then canceled exhibit—although, as we have indicated, the history in colonial settings is one in which colonizers take space from and speak for the colonized, often in ways that the colonized do not recognize as authentic or just. The wrong, in other words, is not only from the possibly lost profit for Indigenous artists; it is also generated by having non-Indigenous artists tell stories, through art, that ought to be told by Indigenous Peoples.

In mounting objections to the use of Indigenous artistic practices by non-Indigenous artists, Indigenous artists face the challenge that their position appears to deny the opportunity for cultural exchange in the domain of artistic practices. Indigenous artists and their advocates respond by acknowledging that the fair exchange of artistic practices will be difficult so long as colonial infrastructure remains in place. But, they assert, even in the current circumstances, artistic exchange is possible and welcome, so long as the conditions that shape it are respectful and fair—rather than ones where non-Indigenous artists simply *take* what they like from Indigenous-produced art without consultation or direct engagement with Indigenous Peoples themselves. Newman emphasizes that artistic exchange must be carried out properly—that is, "Where it's done with accountability. Where it's done from within a relationship within the community."[53] The result is that additional consultation burdens are placed on non-Indigenous artists, like PL and Coleman, if they wish to adopt or profit from traditionally Indigenous forms of art. We will consider forms that this consultation can take in the next chapter.

Wariness with respect to artistic appropriation by non-Indigenous artists is connected to recent efforts to dismantle a fourth and especially egregious type of appropriation in the form of non-Indigenous peoples laying claim to Indigeneity itself—people known, as mentioned earlier, as pretendians or race shifters. Pretendians are individuals with no connection to Indigenous ancestry who masquerade as such, claiming authority to speak on behalf of the Indigenous experience and in so doing taking benefits that are reserved for Indigenous Peoples.

These benefits include access to coveted positions, such as scholarships at universities or employment positions reserved for people with Indigenous ancestry, which are then denied to the Indigenous Peoples for whom they are reserved.[54] The reservation of space for Indigenous individuals is important in settler states that are taking serious steps to engage in restitution toward and reconciliation with those they have wronged. Historically, Indigenous Peoples were both explicitly and implicitly denied opportunities to access higher education, quality employment, political office, and so on. The result is that Indigenous Peoples continue to be underrepresented in all of these spaces and thereby cannot take advantage of the benefits that flow from them, including with respect to additional wealth, status, and respect. Remedying the wrongs of colonialism requires both corrective and distributive justice. Corrective justice focuses on remedying specific injustices inflicted by one person or group on another person or group, and distributive justice revolves around ensuring that the various benefits (financial, mainly, but also with respect to valuable employment and educational opportunities) are distributed fairly. Programs that reserve spaces for Indigenous Peoples contribute to both objectives.[55] Where fraudsters take these spots, no such remedial redistribution takes place.

That denial is a wrong in and of itself, but it generates another, more significant one. In claiming Indigenous identity, pretendians imply a history of trauma and dispossession at the hands of settler states that they do not possess. Especially where pretendians make public statements about their alleged past trauma, they are "exploit[ing] trauma that is not theirs to tell, and ignor[ing] the actual people and communities who constantly struggle with the effects of colonization and trauma to this day."[56] For example, Gina Adams, hired as an allegedly Indigenous artist at Emily Carr University, asserted that her grandfather had been taken from his family to attend a residential school. When such individuals claim the authority to speak and use that authority to tell a false story, less space is given to Indigenous Peoples to tell truthful stories of their past: "Every time they speak as an Indigenous person or for Indigenous people, they are claiming that they have superior knowledge of the Indigenous world. Authentic knowledge coming from real Indigenous people's voices is shunted away from the microphone."[57] Why are pretendians so successful? One scholar explains that such imposters create backgrounds of hardship that sound plausible to outsiders, drawing on "pre-existing Indigenous stereotypes and play[ing] heavily on tropes of family violence, racism and poverty." These stories are believable enough to outsiders that there is no felt need to interrogate the narrative. The choice to appropriate *identity* is in effect the "final act of colonial theft of our very identities and the resources that accompany them."[58]

The task of this chapter has been to outline four distinct ways in which Indigenous Peoples are the victims of cultural appropriation: with respect to artifacts, spiritual practices, artistic practices, and identities. In each of the four instances of appropriation we described, the amplifiers that render acts of appropriation especially wrongful have been present to varying degrees, most strongly with respect to the appropriation of identities: Indigenous Peoples have not consented to any of these forms of appropriation, and Indigenous communities are increasingly vocal about their objections to them; Indigenous Peoples remain in a position of intense vulnerability across settler states; and where these appropriations persist, non-Indigenous peoples are too often the ones who profit financially. These forms of appropriation along with their apparent permissibility all stem from the history of settler colonialism and its attempts at cultural genocide. Settler colonial states made the cultural and spiritual practices of Indigenous Peoples illegal, and having made them so, stole the artifacts that accompanied them on the grounds that they had to be preserved as a kind of memory of a dying race.

Indigenous cultural and spiritual practices are of course no longer illegal, but the long-term impact of these mostly past laws is that many Indigenous Peoples were forced to grow up without connection to their traditions. Indigenous resurgence in part focuses on revitalizing cultural and spiritual practices. It has a clear element of resistance against the legacies of colonialism and its attempts at destroying Indigenous culture, but more important, it is defined by its emphasis on reestablishing healthy, robust, and self-determining Indigenous communities. Coburn writes that resurgence "decentres colonialism by reimagining and re-creating Indigenous worldviews and practices."[59] Its central aim is on the rebuilding of healthy Indigenous relationships; "relationships (or kinship networks)" are "at the core of authentic Indigenous identity."[60]

The legacy of attempted cultural genocide remains, and it continues to make it easy for settler colonialists to appropriate from Indigenous cultures. That same history compels us to evaluate that appropriation from Indigenous cultures more stringently, with a scrutiny that we might not bring to analogous acts of cultural exchange between peoples without that same history. In the next and final chapter, we consider a range of strategies that have been and can be taken by members of dominant communities—states, nongovernmental organizations, private companies, and individuals—to engage respectfully with disadvantaged communities' cultural symbols and practices. These strategies, we argue, are underpinned by a commitment to two principles: respectful collaboration and equitable engagement.

6

MITIGATING WRONGFUL CULTURAL APPROPRIATION

So far in this book, we have offered an account of cultural appropriation, the conditions under which it is significantly wrongful, and how it differs from other forms of cultural engagement, including others that can also be wrongful. In this final chapter, we turn to the next obvious question: If cultural appropriation is wrongful, what should be done?

As we explained in the introduction, critics of cultural appropriation claims typically offer three objections to efforts to restrict, constrain, or even criticize alleged acts of cultural appropriation. The first objection is that what has been described as cultural appropriation is instead just one of many forms of cultural engagement; that cultural engagement is an important—indeed critical—driver of human progress; and therefore that attempts to stop so-called appropriation amount to efforts to hold back the inevitable evolution of humankind. A second objection denies that harm or wrong comes from acts of cultural appropriation and highlights instead the ways in which cultures benefit from it, in particular where the culture from which the appropriation takes place is disadvantaged; sometimes this objection acknowledges the harm but proposes that the benefits far outweigh it. A third objection is crankier, arguing that objections to cultural borrowings are manifestations of identity politics or political correctness gone too far. Those who make these objections typically share the view that attempts to curb cultural appropriation amount to unacceptable freedom-of-speech violations.

Below we will briefly revisit the worry about speech restrictions before turning to an outline of principles that can underpin efforts to avoid cultural appropriation. These principles, we demonstrate, underpin a wide range of existing attempts to avoid cultural appropriation, taken by political, social, and economic actors in democratic societies. These strategies, as we outline, operate to enable the goods of cultural exchange *and* to minimize or even *by* minimizing the wrongs of cultural appropriation. In other words, there are many remedies that are available to those who wish to prioritize both the free exchange of ideas and respect for disadvantaged groups. We examine several remedies, including, with respect to Indigenous Peoples in particular, the legal protection of key cultural elements, and then more generally, profit sharing, the modification of museum curation practices, the altering of arts granting agency practices, and attention to consumer preferences. To preview our conclusion, we demonstrate that it is possible to remedy many of the harms of cultural appropriation while responding plausibly to the set of worries outlined above.

Freedom of Expression and Cultural Appropriation Claims

As we detailed in the introduction, for many of those who are frustrated with claims of cultural appropriation, the pivotal issue is one of freedom of expression. On this view, any attempt to restrict cultural engagement on the grounds that it is appropriative—whether it is intended to produce art or profit—amounts to a violation of freedom of expression. What fashion designers and artists are doing just *is* expressing themselves in ways that ought to be treated as protected speech. This objection was central to the controversy generated by Lionel Shriver, which we considered in the introduction, and it is core to the way that Canadian artists responded to the Canada Council for the Arts' choice to consider whether proposed projects ran the risk of engaging in cultural appropriation as part of its funding protocols, which we consider below.

Freedom of expression must be protected in democratic states. It is, as many scholars of democracy have observed, a bedrock right: Citizens in democracies must be able to use their voice, in public, to consider, contest, and even protest government policy as well as press government into adopting alternative policies that they find preferable. They are permitted to protest in a wide range of public spaces, including newspapers, in front of government buildings, on social media, and so on. Authoritarian states suppress speech as a matter of course, and democracies are distinguished by their commitment to protecting and even enabling it. Where there is disagreement among theorists of democracy is with respect to the scope of free expression. A common example is to say that speech is protected, but that the use of speech to incite violence or panic is not permitted—as, for example, in the oft-cited case of intentionally yelling "fire" in a crowded theater, knowing that there is no fire, and under the condition that a stampede is a possible outcome. That illustration demonstrates that there are conflicting values—in this case, safety—that could be sacrificed if there were no boundaries at all on speech. Democratic states also typically have libel laws, which prohibit making public statements about others that are untrue and that impact how they are treated by others around them, or that damage their reputation. Many states constrain hate speech too—that is, speech that directs hatred at or incites violence toward disadvantaged groups.

One challenge is to distinguish hate speech from other forms of unwelcome speech that may, to the contrary, merit protection. So, for instance, as we described in chapter 1, according to at least some democratic theorists, citizens must be permitted to *ridicule* others, including with respect to their deeply held beliefs and even when doing so is offensive to them.[1] It may be *nicer* to avoid doing so, but it is not outside the boundaries of what ought to be protected by speech. What worries critics of cultural appropriation claims is that restrictions on the use of cultural symbols and practices, which are connected to disadvantaged groups, look more like policing ridicule than protecting these groups from hatred or violence. The inevitable result of this policing is to engage in a form of "censorship [that] hampers creativity and stifles the power of expression."[2] We agree that worries about stifling expression must be taken seriously and aim to show in what follows that there are many ways to respond to cultural appropriation without stifling expression.

The Principles of Respectful Collaboration and Equitable Engagement

In the remainder of the chapter, we offer an account and analysis of several strategies, taken by a wide range of social, economic, and political actors, to avoid cultural appropriation, or in response to claims of wrongful cultural appropriation. What they share is that, for the most part, they do not generally favor or recommend outright bans of appropriative actions—but they do, as a collective, favor respecting two key principles, which we will first outline: respectful collaboration and equitable engagement. There is no single entity with the authority or capacity to ban or allow culturally appropriative acts. The mobs that are sometimes triggered in and by social media, and that are accused of encouraging the so-called cancel culture that we described in the first chapter, do not count as such an authority; while collectively those who participate in these pile-ons can impact which products are sold or which art pieces are made available for viewing, they cannot and do not ban cultural appropriation or allow it to transpire. Rather, actors and individuals from a wide range of political, social, and economic spaces can and do operate so as to avoid cultural appropriation; these actors include the state in a small number of cases, but more frequently they are civil society actors (and private individuals) who aim to act respectfully as they engage with and across cultures, especially with cultures that are disadvantaged in some way.

Where scholars or activists offer ways forward to those who aim to avoid cultural appropriation, respectful collaboration and equitable engagement are frequently invoked. These two principles are often connected in practice, but they each respond to different amplifiers: A commitment to respectful collaboration aims to respond to worries about power imbalances, which can make it hard to assess whether consent has been given, and a commitment to equitable engagement aims to respond to concerns about profit.

A commitment to respectful collaboration requires that parties that appropriate aspects of another's culture, especially (but not only) where that culture is relatively disadvantaged, must "put the work into building cultural knowledge, fostering relationships, and following cultural protocols" so that collaboration can proceed on the basis of trust as well as respect.[3] Diane Lalonde describes one such example in which a media company followed through on this commitment. The Cook Inlet Tribal Council initiated a partnership with a non-Indigenous company, E-Line Media, to produce a video game called (in English) *Never Alone*. *Never Alone* is one of many newly produced Indigenous-themed video games demonstrating that "Indigenous cultures are rich sources for game ideas that can provide players with authentic experiences and viewpoints they may not encounter elsewhere in mainstream culture." These games have multiple objectives: to share "family, historical and traditional stories," "offer hopeful self-expression," and "portray Indigenous storytelling, teachings and ways of knowing for their own people and the wider world."[4]

In the course of developing the video game, one commentator noted that "Cook Inlet Tribal Council members weren't just asked to superficially consult; they became part of a greenlight committee that had equal numbers of E-Line employees and Natives, and worked together to address problems related to everything from concept art to personnel."[5] The result was that over the course of the partnership and extensive consultation, a culturally appropriate storyline and characters were developed, and an Indigenous-owned video game company was created to partner officially with the non-Indigenous organization. When E-Line Media was approached for the partnership, its owner explained that his first move was to look at other Indigenous-themed video games, only to find that the portrayal of Indigenous Peoples was full of caricatured stereotypes. One E-Line representative further stressed that in the company's original game rubric, the villain had been presented as a raven, but consultation with the community led it to change that because while Western culture depicts ravens as harbingers of darkness, in Indigenous cultures, they have a sacredness about them.[6]

A focus on engaging in an equitable manner is also critical to avoiding cultural appropriation. As we detailed in chapter 4, cultural appropriation is particularly harmful when the appropriator profits at the expense of the disadvantaged community that is, as it were, home to a specific practice or symbol. So where profit-making companies aim to generate profit from the cultural goods produced by a disadvantaged community without engaging in harmful appropriation, one key strategy is to find ways to fairly compensate the relevant cultural creators. There are several ways that fair compensation can be arranged.

One is by constructing formal agreements that specifically address compensation and intellectual property, especially within a system of respectful engagement. Compensation can be offered in multiple forms, such as lump-sum payments or with respect to a fair distribution of profits that stem from sales of products. Mexican fashion designer Carla Fernández is well known for her constructive work with Indigenous communities across her country. According to one commentator, Fernández is "famous" for her claim that "the haute couture of Mexico is located in indigenous villages." She works with Indigenous designers through a nongovernmental organization that she coordinates to produce goods for their own communities—goods that will be attractive to tourists and thereby generate profit for them—and along the way gains permission to deploy some of these designs for her haute couture label.[7] In supporting mainly women artisans in Indigenous communities to earn profit from their skills, Fernández is also credited with ensuring that traditional Indigenous techniques for producing goods, which are often done by hand, time-consuming to both learn and engage in, and thereby at risk of disappearance because they are inefficient by corporate standards, can be preserved productively.[8]

Another model is the one adopted by the founder of the Brazilian fashion label Osklen, Oskar Metsavaht. One of his recent collections was inspired by the designs and fabrics of an Indigenous community, the Asháninka, who live in the rainforest in both Brazil and Peru. Metsavaht asked the community for permission to reproduce its designs and use its fabrics in his collection. The community asked for a onetime payment of approximately US$50,000, which was in turn used first to build a school and second to buy a piece of land that allowed for the construction of a space where the tribe was able to sell its own products.[9] In supporting this community to bring its products to market, Metsavaht has also been able to make public the community's struggles to sustain its own way of life—in particular, in the face of illegal loggers, whose operations have threatened the land's ability to support the community.[10]

By adopting the principle of respectful collaboration, which emphasizes the importance of *how* would-be appropriators interact with disadvantage communities, and the principle of equitable engagement, which underscores the significance of a fair distribution of the benefits of would-be appropriation, wrongful cultural appropriation can thereby be avoided. What members of the relevant community require of would-be appropriators is a commitment to interacting in ways in which they are treated as equals, and in which their preferences and needs are given priority—to try to move past the injustices that ordinarily shape how privileged and disadvantaged groups interact.

These ways of engaging have an additional benefit. Many people prefer that the products they consume, or the art that they purchase and display, do not propagate stereotypes, that they indeed support artists and artisans from disadvantaged groups, that the products and art are respectful of the communities from which the material originates, and so on. Among those who are interpreted as desiring to cancel the voices of others are in fact consumers who "are motivated to buy cultural products to connect with others from their communities and as an affirmation of social responsibility." Fernández and Metsavaht demonstrate not only respect for the communities from which they draw their inspiration but also attentiveness to the desire of consumers who are actively "looking for unique and meaningful artisan pieces or those motivated towards affirming their social responsibility and concerns about artisan enterprise and ecological sustainability."[11]

In what follows, we outline strategies that various entities—from governments to nongovernmental organizations and museums—have deployed to avoid wrongful cultural appropriation, and that deliberately aim to take seriously the importance of respectful collaboration and equitable engagement. What respectful collaboration and equitable engagement look like differs in specific cases, according to the motive and objective of the entity that initiates them. These examples will demonstrate that political, social, and economic actors can—if they desire—engage in respectful ways with cultural symbols and practices that originate in disadvantaged communities without impeding freedom of expression.

Legal Protection

We begin with an account of one main way that the state protects against harmful cultural appropriation: via legal protections for Indigenous Peoples' cultural products. For instance, in 2000, Panama adopted a law to protect the rights of Indigenous Peoples with respect to their "traditional knowledge" and "cultural identity." The law's first article lays out its objective:

> To protect the collective intellectual property rights and traditional knowledge of Indigenous Peoples in their creations, such as inventions, models, drawings and designs, innovations contained in the images, figures, symbols, graphics, stone carvings and other details; as well as the cultural elements of their history, music, art and traditional forms of artistic expression suitable for commercial use, via a special system to register, promote and market their rights,

> in order to highlight the social and cultural values of indigenous cultures and guarantee social justice for them.[12]

The act goes on to explain the wide range of protected items, including traditional clothing, musical instruments, dances, performance styles, and traditional artisanal practices. The law outlines that there will be a formal registration process whereby Indigenous Peoples can identify an item or practice for which legal protection is sought. Additionally, the 2007 modifications to the Panamanian criminal code made it illegal to engage in the "reproduction, copying or modification of works or traditional knowledge" of Indigenous Peoples.[13]

Similarly, in the United States, the Indian Arts and Crafts Act prohibits artists or vendors from selling products that misleadingly suggest they have been produced by American Indian tribes. Both individuals and companies can at least in principle face penalties for violating the provisions of the act.[14] Objects covered by the act include pottery, baskets, jewelry, rugs, and clothing.

These kinds of legal protections for Indigenous Peoples aim to respond to their vulnerability—vulnerability created by ongoing settler colonialism. The involvement of the state is at least in part a recognition of what we described in chapter 5—namely, that Indigenous Peoples have been the victims of wrongful cultural appropriation, which, because of the persistence of colonial structures and the systemic injustice that they sustain, they are ill-equipped to protest themselves against. This state-enforced legal protection against some forms of cultural appropriation can therefore be understood as one aspect of the state's attempt to reconcile with Indigenous Peoples.

Such laws acknowledge that arts and crafts, including the materials with which they are made and the manufacturing processes that are deployed to create them, are deeply connected to Indigenous culture and cultural expression. They also acknowledge that the demand for so-called Indigenous products is substantial—and that where individual artists pretend to be Indigenous or where shops misleadingly suggest that certain of their products are Indigenous produced, such individuals and shops are capitalizing on the ignorance of consumers, and in so doing, absorbing profit that ought to go to Indigenous artists and craftspeople. In the United States, the Indian Arts and Crafts Act thereby tries to protect them "against the leveraging of their culture for non-Native-American economic gain."[15]

Here is an example of how the act operates in practice. In 2023, an artist who falsely claimed to be a member of the Nez Perce Tribe was charged with violating the terms of the act. He had been selling Indigenous-style pendants in a local market for nearly ten years when those charged with enforcing the act received a complaint, ultimately confirmed, that the artist was not in fact of Indigenous origin.[16] He was sentenced to eighteen months of probation. Nevertheless, the act has been criticized for lack of enforcement, and at the time of this writing, legislation is being considered that would strengthen enforcement mechanisms to better enable it to do the work it is meant to do. Then secretary of the Department of the Interior Deb Haaland, who is herself a member of the Pueblo of Laguna, explained in supporting more aggressive enforcement legislation that "unfortunately forgery and copies hinder the positive economic opportunities available to Native artists and their families," and correspondingly that "buying authentic pottery, jewelry, mixed-media creations, paintings and other art from Native American artists helps support tribal economies."[17]

In several countries with Indigenous populations, there is additional legal protection offered to "traditional knowledge."[18] Trademark legislation in the United States, for instance, allows for the registration of a wide range of goods, including "names, certain phrases, symbols, designs, artwork, certain music, and characters in oral tradition," subject to some constraints—and in so doing prevents others from, in particular, using these goods in order to make a profit.[19] Using this legislation, the Navajo Nation sued Urban Outfitters for using the term "Navajo" to market a whole range of products—including "navajo hipster panties"—citing the fact that the term had been registered as a trademark in 1943.[20] In the end, the Navajo Nation and Urban Outfitters settled, agreeing to collaborate to coproduce Native jewelry that would be available at the store for sale. Or in an opposite situation, a US court canceled the trademark for the Washington Redskins on the grounds that it was "disparaging" to American Indians.[21]

Ultimately, these forms of legal protection are a response to the knowledge that Indigenous Peoples' cultural goods have been stolen, exploited, and reproduced against their will—and that they have been, without external support, unable to resist these actions. So these legal protections operate as a kind of corrective to enable Indigenous Peoples to better manage and control the ways in which their cultural products are understood as well as used by non-Indigenous peoples. They do not demonstrate respectful collaboration and equitable engagement directly as much as they generate conditions under which such collaboration and engagement are more likely.

Legal protection is a direct way in which states intervene to protect against particularly harmful forms of cultural appropriation. A state can intervene indirectly too. In several of the cases that we consider below, the state takes an active role in shaping how civil society organizations engage with other cultures, especially disadvantaged ones, by providing templates or guidelines that encourage these organizations to engage respectfully, thereby avoiding appropriative actions. We consider both museum construction and curation along with arts granting agencies.

Museum Curation

Museums have been the center of many discussions of cultural appropriation—as, for example, the Karl May Museum in Germany that we described in chapter 4; this museum was accused of cultural appropriation for the way in which it presented objects that are central to Indigenous cultures, the provenance of which were suspect. Museums and their curators have a considerable degree of power that they can exercise when choosing to exhibit or hide specific objects, and in how they present them to visitors: "When it comes to choosing, studying and exhibiting the artifacts of 'others,' museums play a significant role in shaping our sense of others and ourselves and the relations between them."[22] For instance, where African cultures have been presented as "quaint" or "primitive" in European or North American museums, visitors to these museums emerge with an incorrect understanding of those African cultures. In many states, at least some museums are state run or funded, meaning that the government can influence to at least some degree how the material in them is presented. In the Canadian case, for example, the Truth and Reconciliation Commission's "Calls to Action" included a focus on museums and the presentation of Indigenous Peoples in these displays, and asked the federal government to provide funding for a full review of museum practices—something that then transpired, and from which we draw below in outlining best practices for museums going forward.[23]

As we explained earlier, one major complaint against museums that possess cultural art and artifacts in their collections has been that the objects have been acquired in objectionable ways, either because they were stolen or because the conditions under which they were "traded" or "exchanged" were not sufficient to justify the claim that they were acquired fairly. Sometimes the objects being displayed were acquired through theft, so the thieves and later purchasers are therefore not entitled to them: "In each case, some person or community has a right to possess and use an object which is taken by someone who has no right to take it."[24] For example, many African countries are demanding that items acquired by colonial countries be returned to them for display and safekeeping. The French government responded to this demand by returning at least some looted objects to Benin recently.[25] President Emmanuel Macron stated publicly at a visit to the University of Ouagadougou in Burkina Faso that "African heritage cannot solely exist in private collections and European museums," and furthermore that "African heritage must be showcased in Paris but also in Dakar, Lagos and Cotonou."[26]

So museums can remedy one wrong, that of theft, by returning stolen items or items that were acquired in unjust circumstances, where those who offered them cannot reasonably be understood as having done so freely. Then at least the dominant wrong of "object appropriation" is remedied. Not all museums, or countries, are in favor of returning looted or stolen items—and many reasons are offered for this resistance. Some deny the injustice claims, arguing that they were taken under conditions that ought to be understood as fair in some way. More often, the resistance takes the form of worry that the country requesting the return of items does not have sufficient capacity to store, restore, or present these items so that they will be preserved over time. In some cases, this resistance is unjust—but in others it is not. For example, it may reflect the reality that some origin countries or communities do not yet have in place the expertise needed to care for these items if they were returned. It may also be the case that given the sheer volume of objects that were looted and which then found their way into museums, no one is making a demand that they be returned.

In these situations, as in the cases of objects acquired justly, the obligation to present cultural practices and symbols respectfully is present. So a second complaint focuses on the *presentation* of materials rather than the materials themselves. The Canadian Museum for Human Rights, for instance, had been criticized for many years for offering a display of Indigenous Peoples in Canada but refusing to use the term "genocide" to describe the history; it changed tack after the 2015 Canadian Truth and Reconciliation report referred to the residential school system as engaging in cultural genocide.[27] Or take as an example a battle in 1906 between the United Kingdom and a small community, Chibok (in what is now Nigeria), that resisted British colonialism. The British colonial state aimed to punish the town for its raids of British traders and launched a "punitive expedition" against it. Over many days, Chibok residents resisted, shooting poisoned arrows at the colonizers, and it took the British Army nearly three months to fully take control of the town. When it finally did, it collected the arrows and spears that the townspeople used and sent them to a museum in London. These artifacts are not currently on display, but online descriptions of them "make no mention of how the spears got there, nor of the town's resistance against 'punitive' colonisation."[28] The descriptions do not fairly or honestly explain the meaning of these items, nor offer an interpretation that is true to the important anticolonial moment that they represent to those who deployed them and their heirs. The wrong here is in the cultural misrepresentation of these objects, closely connected to their unjust acquisition.

Some museums, in such cases, have pursued alternative strategies to avoid cultural appropriation as well as other cultural wrongs. One that is increasingly adopted is "costewardship," which enables members of disadvantaged groups to "collaboratively steward their belongings, representations of themselves and their intangible cultural heritage held in collections or in material produced, curated, and distributed by the museum."[29] If done well, the costewardship of collections that represent aspects of disadvantaged communities is carried out in consultation with, and in deference to, those communities and how they prefer to be represented. In depicting strategies of costewardship, the Smithsonian guidelines maintain that representatives from the relevant community are to be treated as the "authority" or "cultural custodians" of the material, and that decisions with respect to how to present the material "must be conducted in a spirit of consultation and collaboration"—doing so demonstrates respect for that community.[30] So even if objects cannot be returned to these communities—because a return is not desired or feasible—costewardship ensures that the artifacts are appropriately contextualized and presented in a nonoffensive manner. For example, art historians A. W. Eaton and Ivan Gaskell describe a US museum that displays the content of "sacred bundles" whose origins are in an American Indigenous community—but in that community, these bundles would ordinarily remain closed and their contents known only to those who are charged with protecting them.[31] This latter harm can be avoided by practices of ongoing consultation with the community that is represented.

Arts Granting Agencies

Another available strategy for combating harmful cultural appropriation has been taken by the Canada Council for the Arts, which offers grants to artists to support the production of their work. Since 1992, the council's granting arm has assessed proposed projects for whether they are at risk of engaging in cultural appropriation, specifically when a member of one culture proposes a piece of art in which they would take on the voice or artistic forms that are associated with another cultural group. The objective is not to halt these forms of art from being produced. The council is not claiming that all "appropriated material should be banned or in some way restricted"—an assertion that might "justifiably be called a violation of artistic freedom."[32] The guidelines that support assessing possible projects for whether they engage respectfully with cultural material have been developed with an understanding that while "artistic freedom is an important part of Western culture," it is also the case that government funding decisions can be attentive to the impact of an artistic proposal on disadvantaged communities given its understanding of the specific contextual factors that might shape how the resultant art is received. The guidelines, additionally, encourage artists to engage with minority cultural communities when doing so had not necessarily been part of their original plan. In adopting these guidelines, the council is attempting to be sensitive to the "barriers" that minoritized communities have faced in "speaking on their own behalf," thus leaving the space too open for others to speak for them and to represent them in ways that they do not authorize or even recognize as true to who they are.

One scholar defending the decision to protect minority cultures by being attentive to the dangers of cultural appropriation in art explains that it is neither surprising nor unreasonable for government agencies to account for specific "moral considerations" when allocating money for specific projects. In particular, he says, just as "the Canada Council would be right to reject an aesthetically brilliant story that advocated racial intolerance or hatred of women," it would be right to reject projects that engage in harmful cultural appropriation.[33] According to the council's own description, the goal is to avoid artistic productions that engage in "cultural borrowings or adaptations from a minoritized culture [that] reflect, reinforce or amplify inequalities, stereotypes and historically exploitative relationships that have direct negative consequences on equity-seeking communities in Canada."[34]

At the time that the guidelines were initially adopted, they were met with vigorous opposition from a wide range of Canadian artists reminiscent of recent discourse on avoiding cultural appropriation. The artists collectively published a series of letters to the editor, all gathered under the subheading "Frightening Attack on the Imagination," in one of Canada's national newspapers to share their outrage and annoyance with respect to what they believed was likely to result in unreasonable constraints on artistic expression. Here is Timothy Findley, a well-known Canadian novelist (admittedly one of the author's favorites), articulating his frustration: "I am interested to know what might happen if I were to request support for a novel written in a woman's voice. A child's voice. The voices of men and women and children who lived before my time. A black voice. A murderer's voice. An athlete's voice. A Jew's voice. A fascist's voice. A cat's voice. These are all voices contrary to my own—foreign to my own—and absent in my voice." Bill Driedger wrote,

> If cultural appropriation had never been permitted [composer Giacomo] Puccini could not have written La Boheme, [composer Giuseppe] Verdi's Aida would never have been performed, we would never have thrilled to Laurence Olivier in Hamlet and we would

> have been denied the music of Anna and the King of Siam. Surely the long list of precedents should be enough to stop this latest attempt to discourage our writers, artists and musicians or drive them to more hospitable countries. Such nonsense can only increase contempt for a discredited policy of political correctness.[35]

These complaints (from primarily white artists) interpret the moral requirement to avoid cultural appropriation to mean that they will somehow be restricted to portraying characters who "look" only like themselves, and therefore that the results will be that white male writers are somehow restricted to writing books that describe only white male characters and so on. One consequence of such a view, if it were correct, is that works of literature would in fact be deeply unrepresentative for not including characters from a wide range of backgrounds, being focused on, and indeed limited to, the background of the author. On this interpretation, there is an inevitable tension between artistic freedom and the fair and appropriate inclusion as well as representation of individuals from disadvantaged communities.[36] One scholar observes that these comments come from artists who are inattentive to "the privileges of access to funding, of getting work produced, and of receiving critical attention"; they are used to having their voice *heard* rather than ignored or silenced.[37]

They were, in other words, expressing worries that their own funding would be made less accessible if attention to the portrayal of disadvantaged communities was "policed" or "censored" in some way. For these writers, attention to cultural appropriation amounted to censorship.

Although the path was not smooth, the council remained committed to pursuing an arts environment in Canada in which both access to arts funding and the creation of art (with that funding) fairly includes and represents members of disadvantaged groups. In a recent report, the council focused specifically on how to avoid appropriation with respect to Indigenous Peoples in Canada. Artists or organizations that apply to the council for funding, and whose proposals in some way connect to Indigenous history, stories, or other artistic traditions, must demonstrate that they have made tangible efforts to "engage with artists or other members of the Indigenous communities whose culture or protocols are" represented by the proposed project.[38] The council is clear that the explanations offered by artists are not formally scored but rather that they feature in the conversation that jury members have with respect to the proposed project. Moreover, the council works with Indigenous staff members when concerns are raised about specific proposals. The goal is to encourage and protect respectful engagement between artists from dominant cultures and minority, disadvantaged cultures.

Going Forward

The worry about cultural appropriation claims is that they are deployed to "cancel" others—that is, to suppress what they ought to be permitted to say and express in public. In other words, this argument says that what some people call cultural appropriation is a form of speech that warrants protection. This assertion is powerful since the ability to express oneself in public space is a key right in democratic states; as we noted earlier, censorship is attributed to authoritarian states, which do not permit citizens to speak in opposition to or critically of the government. Others maintain not that appropriation per se warrants protection but instead that any attempt to limit it will generate more difficulties than benefits. A particular worry is that if the "state" were to intervene, it would do so clumsily; this objection is a generalized worry that the only way for the state to act is bluntly in ways that would, ultimately, stifle speech. What the strategies we have described above show, however, is that there are many ways in which entities and agencies—some but not all connected to the state—can operate while avoiding cultural appropriation, without suppressing speech.

On the contrary, what is striking about so many of the examples that we have considered in the discussion above with respect to how to avoid wrongful cultural appropriation is that in fact they *support* rather than undermine freedom of expression. They do so by making space for the voice of disadvantaged communities, which has historically been ignored or suppressed. When the Canada Council for the Arts offers grant money to projects that engage with members of disadvantaged groups or specially selects artists from disadvantaged groups for funding, what it is consciously doing is opening space for individuals whose voices have been silenced or sidelined in the past to make their voices heard. The same is true when museums engage in the costewardship of collections with disadvantaged groups: The *goal* is to ensure that members of these groups tell their *own* story and represent themselves in ways that they recognize as truthful.

This freedom-of-expression benefit is sometimes ignored by members of more privileged groups; that is what was striking about the significant negative response to the Canada Council for the Arts guidelines. Those with a negative response were dominated by members of privileged groups, who worried that artists (including themselves) would be silenced because of the council's attention to the representation of disadvantaged groups. Yet artistic freedom of expression is not a zero-sum game. It can seem that way, for example, when a funding agency creates separate funding streams to support minority voices (although we would argue that such is not the situation), but in the case at issue, with respect to funding artistic creations that are appropriately respectful of other cultures, it is simply a

Artistic freedom of expression is not a zero-sum game.

matter of ensuring that artists meet certain "respect" requirements to gain access to funding. No one is silenced or denied the opportunity to produce their own art (for instance, non-Indigenous artists who work within an Indigenous context are still funded—if they can demonstrate that they are working collaboratively and respectfully with Indigenous communities), and fair funding criteria elevate less privileged voices in ways that are consistent with and support the freedom of expression that is key to democratic states.

CONCLUSION

In general, we believe that going forward, there are three important lessons to be learned from the strategies of respectful collaboration and equitable engagement that we have considered above. One is that consultation and (where relevant) coproduction with disadvantaged groups does not translate into violations of freedom of expression. On the contrary, as we noted in the conclusion to chapter 6, the forms of consultation and coproduction we discussed, which are informed by the principles of respectful collaboration and equitable engagement, support freedom of expression by offering space for and protecting the voices of disadvantaged groups.

A second lesson is that it is possible to reach out to and engage with members of disadvantaged groups to avoid harmful cultural appropriation; there will always be questions about to whom to reach out, who represents the views of the group, which symbols and practices are those that merit protection or are central to a group's identity, and so on. But these difficulties are surmountable with reasonable amounts of effort—and by "surmountable," we do not mean that it will be possible to please everyone. Critics, in most cases, will remain. Rather, we mean to highlight several processes that can be undertaken to engage disadvantaged groups that can allow creators to defend their choices against critics in ways that are meaningful—namely, that ought to be able to satisfy those who object to cultural appropriation. One advantage here is that many consumers are keen to know that the goods they purchase are authentic, so that for-profit entities have a financial interest in producing goods that avoid harmful cultural appropriation.

A third and final lesson, which we draw from the analysis that we have developed in this book, is that many examples of cultural appropriation are indeed trivial in the sense that they do not generate significant wrong. But some of them do, and these we must guard against as part of the multicultural democratic project, which aims at inclusion *of all* on full and equal terms.

These lessons make sense for institutions or larger-scale organizations that have the power to shape the way in which disadvantaged groups are represented in public space. They are lessons that, if learned, can enable such institutions to engage respectfully with cultural products in ways that are to the benefit of those who are disadvantaged, bringing advantage to them as well as to citizens more generally. At the same time, engaging in these forms of respectful collaboration does not, as we have said, constrain or restrict freedom of expression.

Still, how do these lessons apply to individuals, one might ask? It is fine to suggest that larger organizations should engage with key representatives of disadvantaged cultures so as to ensure that their symbols and practices are respectfully presented, and that such cultures remain in charge of what that respectful presentation looks like. Yet what does our analysis mean for individuals who may appreciate the kimono or cheongsam? Are they permitted to wear these items of clothing without being accused of cultural appropriation? Can they rightly claim that they are *appreciating* these cultural items rather than appropriating them? Are they permitted to own and display cultural items in their home if they are not members of those cultures?

The short answer is yes, individuals can wear these items of clothing and display cultural items—without in general opening themselves up to (valid) claims that they are engaging in unacceptable cultural appropriation. Where they are purchasing cultural items, they should certainly attempt to do so directly from the members of the culture themselves—or in ways that generate benefits for them. When they are wearing clothing styles that have their origin in cultures that are not their own, they, too, can be attentive to their historical meaning, and ensure that they understand how and where the culture uses these particular items of clothing. If individuals wear kimonos or cheongsams, they can be asked to understand something about the clothing item and the culture from which it stems as a condition for doing so morally. In chapter 3, we described culpable ignorance as one feature of cultural appropriation, and that is relevant here: Individuals living in multicultural societies should be able to recognize that certain clothing items are tied to specific cultures, that they may have meaning to those cultures, and that in choosing them, they ought to be aware of what they are choosing. But sometimes they will not be; they may be genuinely ignorant of these histories, even though they ought to be aware of them. In those cases, respectful individuals will respond to worries and objections to their choices with a willingness to learn more about the symbols and practices that they have unknowingly borrowed, and with an openness to choosing against engaging with them if doing so is wrong or otherwise offensive.

More specifically, some cultural items and clothing pieces may reasonably be "claimed" by a culture as unavailable for outsiders to use; typically, these items will have to do with their spiritual or sacred practices. That is, it is permissible and legitimate for cultures to ask others to leave their spiritual items alone out of respect for their sacred practices. Individuals cannot be prevented in any formal way from violating these preferences and requests. We are not suggesting that authorities become involved when nongroup members choose to wear or engage with items that have spiritual significance. All that we are saying is that individuals can reasonably be asked to avoid doing so as part of respectful and civil engagement with members of all cultures, including disadvantaged ones. Suggesting that individuals engage respectfully with the cultural material of others is not a restriction of their speech, and indeed it is not even a restriction on their actions. It is a proposal for a way to engage in multicultural societies that are rife with inequalities, which often follow religious, cultural, and racial lines.

Our book has attempted to intervene in current discussions of cultural appropriation. We have waded into a wide range of conversations and disagreements about what counts as cultural appropriation, whether it is wrong, and what should be done about it. We have done so as scholars of multiculturalism who believe that societies are richer when they are more diverse, and who also recognize that citizens and residents of multicultural societies must learn how to engage with each other's cultural differences in ways that are respectful rather than insulting. In our view, multicultural political theory has more to do—and we have contributed to this project—to elaborate how citizens of diverse cultural backgrounds can and should interact with each other.[1]

We began with a definition of cultural appropriation as the nonconsensual taking by one group of valuable cultural symbols or practices that belong to another culture, when the taking group does or should know better than to do so. Ours is a normative account of cultural appropriation, according to which it is prima facie wrong to engage in it—but, we said, many acts of cultural appropriation are trivial, including many in the food and musical space. We distinguished cultural appropriation from other forms of harmful cultural engagement, including misrepresentation and offense, both of which (along with cultural appropriation) demonstrate a lack of respect for others. And then to better interpret acts of cultural appropriation as significantly or merely trivially wrongful, we suggested that the wrongfulness of such acts tracks with key amplifiers—namely, the presence of power imbalances and profit making at the expense of disadvantaged groups. In our penultimate chapter, we showed that all forms of wrongful cultural engagements are directed at Indigenous Peoples, who are the victims of egregious forms of cultural appropriation and are owed protection from it as part of the settler attempt to remedy the ongoing harms of colonialism. Finally, we outlined a wide range of actions taken by political, economic, and social entities in democratic communities that operate to remedy the wrongs of cultural appropriation—actions that, we argued, not only do not violate freedom of expression but on the contrary further enable it by opening more and better space for disadvantaged citizens to express themselves freely.

We started this book with two objectives, one theoretical and one practical. Having opened with the observation that the political theory of multiculturalism has not engaged sufficiently with how citizens and residents in diverse democracies can and should engage with each other respectfully, our theoretical objective has been to map out the terrain of cultural appropriation and distinguish it from other forms of disrespectful cultural engagement. Political theory has sometimes appeared to suggest that were democracies to find remedies for the racism and other forms of injustice that permeate them, racial, cultural, and ethnic conflicts would disappear along with them. Our view is a kind of "both-and"; we of course agree that democracies must continue to seek ways to remedy injustice, including racial injustice, and we also believe that a focus on how to engage in respectful conversations around racial and cultural values and identities is part of this project. This theoretical objective underpins the urgent practical one that has also motivated this book—that is, the sense that public discourse in democratic states is increasingly filled with conflicts around ethnic, racial, and cultural values and identities. These conflicts devolve too quickly into canceling or accusations that speech is being restricted. It is likely that our readers will disagree with how we have adjudicated specific cases, and that is okay.

Our hope is not to have gotten the cases *right* such that we reach agreement on all of them. Instead, our hope is that we have constructed a framework that allows for a calm and nuanced account of cultural appropriation, and when it might plausibly be interpreted as wrong, which in turn can reduce cultural conflicts and support productive conversations about how to engage constructively together as a diverse citizenry.

ACKNOWLEDGMENTS

I owe many thanks to many friends and colleagues who have engaged with me on the ideas and text of this book. Most important, I owe thanks to my cocreator, Peter Balint, with whom I first tackled the difficult questions around cultural appropriation—not only what it is but, crucially, what should be done about it and by whom.

Thank you to the reviewers for the MIT Press, who read both the proposal and the full manuscript, and offered helpful comments. Thank you to Karl Widerquist for helping us to navigate the early stages of proposing our work to the MIT Press. My gratitude also goes to my neighbor and colleague Jim Davies and my partner, Jacob J. Krich, who both read the full manuscript and offered extensive thoughts and comments. Engaging with them has made our core claims stronger and, I hope, more persuasive. Thank you to the many people with whom Peter and I have together and separately discussed ideas in this book: Miriam Bankovsky, Jonathan Floyd, Rainer Forst, Margaret Moore, Alasia Nuti, Phil Parvin, and Christine Straehle. To those who chatted with Peter about this book and the ideas in it, but who are not mentioned here, I offer my appreciation to you as well.

Thanks, as always, to my sweet girls, Elisa and Gavi, who made it as clear as possible that while there is nothing interesting about the philosophical dimensions of cultural appropriation, they do appreciate cultural sharing in the form of easily accessible Thai and Indian food. They do not mind who prepares it, as long as it is good.

GLOSSARY

Cancel culture
A set of tactics that deploy social pressure to chastise and even banish (from public spaces) someone who has engaged in offensive actions or made offensive statements.

Culpable ignorance
Ignorance of facts of which, for many possible reasons, one ought already to have been aware.

Cultural appropriation
The knowing or culpably ignorant taking of cultural symbols or practices of significant value to others without their consent, and often against their explicit request to do otherwise.

Cultural engagement
An exchange of cultural ideas and practices on generally equal terms by which individuals gain knowledge about other cultures.

Cultural genocide
A form of genocide that has as its goal the destruction of cultural groups, which is pursued by the deliberate and violent targeting of those groups' cultural practices and symbols, such as by rendering them illegal.

Cultural misrecognition
The failure to respect or understand the cultural practices and symbols of minorities, which translates into treating these practices and symbols carelessly or with disregard.

Cultural misrepresentation
Offering a false or misleading account of another person's cultural artifacts, symbols, or practices.

Cultural offense
An insult or disregard directed at a culture's practices, artifacts, or symbols.

Culture
Norms, practices, interests, and values that characterize distinct groups.

Culture war
A conflict between social and sometimes political groups that are defined by distinctive and opposite cultural values, each of which desires that their own values and beliefs dominate.

Disadvantage
An unfavorable position relative to others so that disadvantaged groups are groups of citizens and residents who experience challenges in accessing goods and services that other groups or citizens and residents do not similarly experience.

Equitable engagement
A form of engagement that is marked by attention to the potential for unjust profit making and distribution, and a desire to ensure that profit from "cultural appropriation" is distributed fairly.

Extractive colonialism
A form of colonialism that is marked by colonizers whose main objective is to exploit the natural resources on a colony's territory.

Freedom of expression
The freedom to express beliefs, thoughts, and opinions in public spaces, and to receive those of others in return, without fear of legal or political penalty.

Harm (versus wrong)
Someone has harmed another if they have damaged their interests in some way, such that they are worse off than they would otherwise have been.

Misrepresentation
Offering a false or misleading account of another person.

Multiculturalism
The political and moral requirement to adopt accommodations that enable minorities of all kinds to participate in the main institutions of society, including social, economic, and political, on equal terms.

Offense
A form of insult or disregard.

Privilege
In the context of cultural appropriation, the position of those in power who can opt to appropriate (or not) the cultural symbols and practices of others with impunity.

Respectful collaboration
A form of collaboration that is marked by the development of respectful relations and the conditions under which they can persist. In the context of "cultural appropriation," such collaboration requires that "appropriators" demonstrate an awareness of power imbalances and consent.

Settler colonialism
A form of colonialism that is marked by the migration of citizens from (historically) largely European countries to conquered "colonies," where Indigenous populations are displaced and dispossessed.

White ignorance
Ignorance demonstrated by "white" people, manifest in a lack of knowledge of or attention to the ways in which dominant institutional structures persistently and pervasively disadvantage minorities.

Wrong (versus harm)
Someone has wronged another if they fail to respect their moral equality, often but not always in the form of violating their rights.

NOTES

Chapter 1

1. Michael Levenson, "Kansas City Chiefs Ban Headdresses at Stadium," Sports, *New York Times*, August 20, 2020, https://www.nytimes.com/2020/08/20/sports/football/Kansas-City-Chiefs-Ban-Headdresses-Face-Paint.html.
2. David Waldstein, "Cleveland Indians Will Abandon Chief Wahoo Logo Next Year," Sports, *New York Times*, January 29, 2018, https://www.nytimes.com/2018/01/29/sports/baseball/cleveland-indians-chief-wahoo-logo.html.
3. Hayley Munguia, "The 2,128 Native American Mascots People Aren't Talking About," *FiveThirtyEight* (blog), September 5, 2014, https://fivethirtyeight.com/features/the-2128-native-american-mascots-people-arent-talking-about/.
4. Emma Bowman, "For Many Native Americans, the Washington Commanders' New Name Offers Some Closure," Race, NPR, February 6, 2022, https://www.npr.org/2022/02/06/1078571919/washington-commanders-name-change-native-americans. For a history of the term, see J. Gordon Hylton, "Why Is the Word 'Redskin' So Offensive?," *Marquette University Law School Faculty Blog*, December 1, 2013, https://law.marquette.edu/facultyblog/2013/12/why-is-the-word-redskin-so-offensive/.
5. Erik Brady, "Daniel Snyder Says Redskins Will Never Change Name," *USA TODAY*, May 9, 2013, https://www.usatoday.com/story/sports/nfl/redskins/2013/05/09/washington-redskins-daniel-snyder/2148127/.
6. Brakkton Booker, "After Mounting Pressure, Washington's NFL Franchise Drops Its Team Name," NPR, July 13, 2020, https://www.npr.org/sections/live-updates-protests-for-racial-justice/2020/07/13/890359987/after-mounting-pressure-washingtons-nfl-franchise-drops-its-team-name.
7. Waldstein, "Cleveland Indians Will Abandon Chief Wahoo Logo Next Year."
8. Vincent Schilling, "How the Kansas City Chiefs Got Their Name and the Boy Scout Tribe of Mic-O-Say," *Indian Country Today News*, September 21, 2019, https://ictnews.org/news/how-the-kansas-city-chiefs-got-their-name-and-the-boy-scout-tribe-of-mic-o-say.
9. Debra Utacia Krol, "With Chiefs in the Super Bowl, Some Native People Say It's Time to Erase the Offensive Name," *USA TODAY*, February 10, 2023, https://www.usatoday.com/story/sports/2023/02/10/native-activists-kansas-city-chiefs-name-mascot-change/11227316002/.

10. John Eligon, "Celebrating the Kansas City Chiefs, the Chop Divides," Sports, *New York Times*, January 29, 2020, https://www.nytimes.com/2020/01/29/sports/football/chiefs-tomahawk-chop.html.

11. Krol, "With Chiefs in the Super Bowl, Some Native People Say It's Time to Erase the Offensive Name."

12. Emma Rothberg, "Biography: Amanda Blackhorse," National Women's History Museum, accessed July 18, 2023, https://www.womenshistory.org/education-resources/biographies/amanda-blackhorse.

13. Krol, "With Chiefs in the Super Bowl, Some Native People Say It's Time to Erase the Offensive Name."

14. Heather Davidson, "How Racism Against Native People Is Normalized, from Mascots to Costumes," *Teen Vogue*, October 31, 2018, https://www.teenvogue.com/story/how-racism-against-native-people-is-normalized-from-mascots-to-costumes.

15. ASU News, "As Football Season Returns, so Does Sports Name Controversy," ASU News, September 6, 2018, https://news.asu.edu/20180906-global-engagement-football-season-returns-so-does-sports-name-controversy.

16. Davidson, "How Racism Against Native People Is Normalized."

17. Lisa Flam, "H&M Pulls Native-Inspired Headdress after Customer Complaints," *TODAY*, August 12, 2013, http://www.today.com/style/h-m-pulls-native-inspired-headdress-after-customer-complaints-6C10900100.

18. Adrienne Keene, "But Why Can't I Wear a Hipster Headdress?," *Native Appropriations* (blog), April 27, 2010, https://nativeappropriations.com/2010/04/but-why-cant-i-wear-a-hipster-headdress.html.

19. Davidson, "How Racism Against Native People Is Normalized."

20. "APA Resolution Recommending the Immediate Retirement of American Indian Mascots, Symbols, Images, and Personalities by Schools, Colleges, Universities, Athletic Teams, and Organizations," American Psychological Association, 2005, https://www.apa.org/about/policy/mascots.pdf.

21. Zack Stanton, "How Native American Team Names Distort Your Psychology," *Politico*, July 16, 2020, https://www.politico.com/news/magazine/2020/07/16/native-american-team-names-psychology-effect-redskins-indians-sports-logos-366409; Stephanie A. Fryberg et al., "Of Warrior Chiefs and Indian Princesses: The Psychological Consequences of American Indian Mascots," *Basic and Applied Social Psychology* 30, no. 3 (September 26, 2008): 208–218, https://doi.org/10.1080/01973530802375003.

22. Allison Torres Burkta, "Native American Mascots—Honoring Culture or Symbol of Disrespect?," Global Sport Matters, April 24, 2018, https://globalsport

matters.com/culture/2018/04/24/native-american-mascots-honoring-culture-symbol-disrespect/.

23. Chu Kim-Prieto et al., "Effect of Exposure to an American Indian Mascot on the Tendency to Stereotype a Different Minority Group," *Journal of Applied Social Psychology* 40, no. 3 (2010): 534–553, https://doi.org/10.1111/j.1559-1816.2010.00586.x.

24. This discussion draws on Seth Lazar, "The Nature and Disvalue of Injury," *Res Publica* 15, no. 3 (2009): 289–304; F. M. Kamm, "Harms, Wrongs, and Meaning in a Pandemic," *Philosophers' Magazine* (blog), 2021, https://philosophersmag.com/harms-wrongs-and-meaning-in-a-pandemic/.

25. Margaret Cho, "Harajuku Girls," October 31, 2005, https://margaretcho.com/2005/10/31/harajuku-girls/.

26. Mihi Ahn, "Gwenihana," Culture, *Salon*, April 10, 2005, https://www.salon.com/2005/04/09/geisha_2/.

27. Adam Wallis, "Gwen Stefani Defends 'Harajuku Girls' Era, Denies Cultural Appropriation," *Global News*, November 20, 2019, https://globalnews.ca/news/6193310/gwen-stefani-defends-harajuku-girls-denies-cultural-appropriation/.

28. Andrew Foote, "Yoga Class Cancelled at University of Ottawa over 'Cultural Issues,'" CBC, November 22, 2015, https://www.cbc.ca/news/canada/ottawa/university-ottawa-yoga-cultural-sensitivity-1.3330441.

29. Scott McLaughlan, "A Brief History of Modern Yoga," *Collector*, July 5, 2022, https://www.thecollector.com/history-of-yoga/.

30. Nadia Gilani, "I Teach Yoga—Its Appropriation by the White Wellness Industry Is a Form of Colonialism, but We Can Move On," *Guardian*, January 3, 2023, https://www.theguardian.com/commentisfree/2023/jan/03/yoga-white-wellness-industry-21st-century-colonialism.

31. Caitlyn Terra, "Cultural Appropriation in Fashion: What Is It and Can It Be Prevented?," *FashionUnited* (blog), October 22, 2021, https://fashionunited.uk/news/culture/cultural-appropriation-in-fashion-what-is-it-and-can-it-be-prevented/2021102258654.

32. Amy Qin, "Teenager's Prom Dress Stirs Furor in U.S.—but Not in China," World, *New York Times*, May 2, 2018, https://www.nytimes.com/2018/05/02/world/asia/chinese-prom-dress.html.

33. Jeremiah Castle, "New Fronts in the Culture Wars? Religion, Partisanship, and Polarization on Religious Liberty and Transgender Rights in the United States," *American Politics Research* 47, no. 3 (May 1, 2019): 650–679, https://doi.org/10.1177/1532673X18818169.

34. Pippa Norris, "Cancel Culture: Myth or Reality?," *Political Studies* 71, no. 1 (February 1, 2023): 148, https://doi.org/10.1177/00323217211037023.

35. Edwin J. Gasque, "Censorship in Art: Preserving Culture or Infringing on Freedom of Expression?," *Medium* (blog), July 28, 2023, https://medium.com/@gasqueedwin/censorship-in-art-preserving-culture-or-infringing-on-freedom-of-expression-115cdbc9568f.

36. Robin J. Ely, Debra Meyerson, and Martin N. Davidson, "Rethinking Political Correctness," *Harvard Business Review*, September 1, 2006, https://hbr.org/2006/09/rethinking-political-correctness.

37. For a discussion of identity in politics, see Avigail Eisenberg, *Reasons of Identity: A Normative Guide to the Political and Legal Assessment of Identity Claims* (Oxford: Oxford University Press, 2009).

38. For discussions of this, see Will Kymlicka, "The Rise and Fall of Multiculturalism? New Debates on Inclusion and Accommodation in Diverse Societies," in *The Multiculturalism Backlash: European Discourses, Policies and Practices*, ed. Steven Vertovec and Susanne Wessendorf (London: Routledge, 2010), 32–49; Steven Vertovec and Susanne Wessendorf, eds., *The Multicultural Backlash: European Discourses, Policies and Practices* (London: Routledge, 2010).

39. Brian Barry, *Culture and Equality: An Egalitarian Critique of Multiculturalism* (Cambridge, MA: Harvard University Press, 2001).

40. Ronald Dworkin, "The Right to Ridicule," *New York Review of Books* 53, no. 5 (March 23, 2006).

41. Joseph H. Carens, "Free Speech and Democratic Norms in the Danish Cartoons Controversy," *International Migration* 44, no. 5 (2006): 33–42.

42. John Stuart Mill, "On Liberty," in *On Liberty and Other Essays*, ed. John Gray (1859; repr., Oxford: Oxford University Press, 1998).

43. That said, the political Right similarly demands that certain practices and symbols be respected; for example, the Right typically objects to flag burning as disrespectful, whereas the Left defends flag burning in terms of freedom of expression.

44. Lionel Shriver, "I Hope the Concept of Cultural Appropriation Is a Passing Fad," *The Guardian*, September 13, 2016, https://www.theguardian.com/commentisfree/2016/sep/13/lionel-shrivers-full-speech-i-hope-the-concept-of-cultural-appropriation-is-a-passing-fad.

45. Will Kymlicka, *Multicultural Citizenship: A Liberal Theory of Minority Rights* (Oxford: Oxford University Press, 1996); Sarah Song, *Justice, Gender and the Politics of Multiculturalism* (Cambridge: Cambridge University Press, 2007); Anne Phillips, *Multiculturalism Without Culture* (Princeton, NJ: Princeton University Press, 2007).

46. Patti Tamara Lenard, "Culture," Stanford Encyclopedia of Philosophy Archive, December 2, 2020, https://plato.stanford.edu/archives/win2020

/entries/culture/; Peter Balint and Patti Tamara Lenard, *Debating Multiculturalism: Should There Be Minority Rights?* (Oxford: Oxford University Press, 2022); Jacob Levy, *Multiculturalism of Fear* (Oxford: Oxford University Press, 2000); Alan Patten, *Equal Recognition: The Moral Foundations of Minority Rights* (Princeton, NJ: Princeton University Press, 2014).

47. John Rawls, *Justice as Fairness: A Restatement* (Cambridge, MA: Belknap Press, 2001).

48. Nils Holtug, *The Politics of Social Cohesion: Immigration, Community, and Justice* (Oxford: Oxford University Press, 2021); Markus Crepaz, *Trust Beyond Borders: Immigration, the Welfare State, and Identity in Modern Societies* (Ann Arbor: University of Michigan Press, 2007).

49. Patti Tamara Lenard, *Trust, Democracy and Multicultural Challenges* (University Park: Penn State University Press, 2012).

50. Jeff Spinner-Halev, "Cultural Pluralism and Partial Citizenship," in *Multicultural Questions*, ed. Christian Joppke and Steven Lukes (Oxford: Oxford University Press, 1999), 65–84.

Chapter 2

1. Ronald Dworkin, "The Right to Ridicule," *New York Review of Books* 53, no. 5 (March 23, 2006); Tariq Modood et al., "The Danish Cartoon Affair: Free Speech, Racism, Islamism, and Integration," *International Migration* 44, no. 5 (2006): 3–62, https://doi.org/10.1111/j.1468-2435.2006.00386.x; Matthew Moran, "Terrorism and the *Banlieues*: The *Charlie Hebdo* Attacks in Context," *Modern & Contemporary France* 25, no. 3 (July 3, 2017): 315–332, https://doi.org/10.1080/09639489.2017.1323199.

2. Dworkin, "The Right to Ridicule."

3. Flemming Rose, "Why I Published Those Cartoons," *Washington Post*, February 19, 2006, http://www.washingtonpost.com/wp-dyn/content/article/2006/02/17/AR2006021702499.html.

4. Patti Tamara Lenard, "Anti-Immigrant Populism and the Duty of Respectful Engagement," in *Minority Rights and Liberal Democratic Insecurities: The Challenge of Unstable Orders*, ed. Anna-Mária Bíró and Dwight Newman (New York: Taylor & Francis, 2022), 117–134.

5. Philip S. S. Howard, "The Problem with Blackface," *Conversation* (blog), June 11, 2018, http://theconversation.com/the-problem-with-blackface-97987.

6. Jonathan Montpetit, "Blackface Stunt Backfires at Montreal University Frosh-Week Event," *Global News*, September 15, 2011, https://globalnews.ca/news/155216/blackface-stunt-backfires-at-montreal-university-frosh-week-event/.

7. Jeremy Helligar, "10 Examples of Cultural Appropriation You Never Thought About," *Reader's Digest* (blog), February 14, 2023, https://www.rd.com/list/examples-of-cultural-appropriation/.

8. Doug Criss, "Here's a List of Celebs and Lawmakers Who Got in Trouble over Blackface," CNN, February 6, 2019, https://www.cnn.com/politics/live-news/virginia-politics-chaos-2019/index.html.

9. "Blackface Stunt Backfires at Université de Montréal."

10. Shaun King, "Eddie Murphy Got It Right in 1984 SNL Skit on White Privilege," *Daily News*, April 9, 2018, https://www.nydailynews.com/2015/10/23/king-eddie-murphy-got-it-right-in-1984-snl-skit-on-white-privilege/.

11. Patti Tamara Lenard, "A Quran Burns, What's Next?," *Free Voice*, July 31, 2023, https://shuddhashar.com/a-quran-burns-whats-next/.

12. Lawrence Blum, "Stereotyping and Stereotypes," in *The International Encyclopedia of Ethics* (Hoboken, NJ: John Wiley & Sons, 2020), 1, 3, https://doi.org/10.1002/9781444367072.wbiee926.

13. Pavan Acharya, "The Dangers of Cultural Misrepresentation in Media," *Drops of Ink* (blog), April 22, 2021, https://www.lhsdoi.com/21631/opinion/the-dangers-of-cultural-misrepresentation-in-media/.

14. Blum, "Stereotyping and Stereotypes," 2.

15. Erich Hatala Matthes, "Cultural Appropriation Without Cultural Essentialism?," *Social Theory and Practice* 42, no. 2 (2016): 343–366; Margaret Moore, "Liberal Nationalism and the Challenge of Essentialism," in *Liberal Nationalism and Its Critics: Normative and Empirical Questions*, ed. Gina Gustavsson and David Miller (Oxford: Oxford University Press, 2020); Tariq Modood, "Anti-Essentialism, Multiculturalism and the 'Recognition' of Religious Groups," *Journal of Political Philosophy* 6, no. 4 (1998): 378–399.

16. Blum, "Stereotyping and Stereotypes," 3. See also Lawrence Blum, "Stereotypes and Stereotyping: A Moral Analysis," *Philosophical Papers* 33, no. 3 (2004): 261–265, https://doi.org/10.1080/05568640409485143.

17. Evi Taylor et al., "The Historical Perspectives of Stereotypes on African-American Males," *Journal of Human Rights and Social Work* 4, no. 3 (September 1, 2019): 213, https://doi.org/10.1007/s41134-019-00096-y.

18. For a general discussion, see Elizabeth A. Bates et al., "The Impact of Gendered Stereotypes on Perceptions of Violence: A Commentary," *Sex Roles* 81, no. 1 (July 1, 2019): 34–43, https://doi.org/10.1007/s11199-019-01029-9.

19. Maria Garcia, "Please Don't Wear a Sombrero: What Cinco De Mayo Really Means, from a Mexican," WBUR, May 2, 2019, https://www.wbur.org/news/2019/05/02/cinco-de-mayo-from-a-mexican.

20. Native Max, "What Cinco de Mayo Is and How to Celebrate It Respectfully," *Native Max Magazine*, May 5, 2018, https://nativemaxmagazine.com/what-cinco-de-mayo-is-and-how-to-celebrate-it-respectfully/.
21. Charles Taylor, *Multiculturalism and the "Politics of Recognition"* (Princeton, NJ: Princeton University Press, 1994).
22. Hilary Pilkington and Necla Acik, "Not Entitled to Talk: (Mis)recognition, Inequality and Social Activism of Young Muslims," *Sociology* 54, no. 1 (February 1, 2020): 181–198, https://doi.org/10.1177/0038038519867630; John Rawls, *A Theory of Justice*, rev. ed. (Cambridge, MA: Belknap Press, 1999).

Chapter 3

1. James O. Young, "Profound Offense and Cultural Appropriation," *Journal of Aesthetics and Art Criticism* 63, no. 2 (2005): 136.
2. Paul Raffaele, "Man-Eaters of Tsavo," *Smithsonian Magazine*, January 2010, https://www.smithsonianmag.com/science-nature/man-eaters-of-tsavo-11614317/.
3. Miranda Moure, "9 Famous Stolen Artifacts That Are Still on Display in Museums Today," Matador Network, July 20, 2020, https://matadornetwork.com/read/stolen-artifacts-museums/.
4. "Sarees Go Global as Oprah, Lady Gaga Drape Themselves," *BW Businessworld*, November 8, 2014, http://businessworld.in/article/Sarees-Go-Global-As-Oprah-Lady-Gaga-Drape-Themselves/08-11-2014-62308.
5. There is also much commentary from those external to Islam about the merits of the hijab or burka, much of which connects antifeminist meaning to these forms of dress. For an analysis of the hijab in political life, see Cécile Laborde, *Critical Republicanism: The Hijab Controversy and Political Philosophy* (Oxford: Oxford University Press, 2008).
6. Monique Deveaux, "A Deliberative Approach to Conflicts of Culture," *Political Theory* 31, no. 6 (December 1, 2003): 780–807, https://doi.org/10.1177/0090591703256685.
7. Nor does it mean that such circumstances are static. It is possible to imagine circumstances where Greek or Italian citizens begin to express concern that their historical symbols are being culturally appropriated, which others then ought to take seriously.
8. Jason Baird Jackson, "On Cultural Appropriation," *Journal of Folklore Research* 58, no. 1 (April 2021): 88, https://doi.org/10.2979/jfolkrese.58.1.04.
9. Samantha Schmidt, "'It's Just a Dress': Teen's Chinese Prom Outfit Spurs Storm of 'Cultural Appropriation' Outrage," *National Post*, May 2, 2018, https://

nationalpost.com/news/world/its-just-a-dress-teens-chinese-prom-outfit-spurs-storm-of-cultural-appropriation-outrage.

10. Leah Prinzivalli, "Selma Blair Is Being Accused of Cultural Appropriation for Wearing a Turban," *Allure*, June 3, 2019, https://www.allure.com/story/selma-blair-turban-cultural-appropriation-accusations.

11. Allyson Chiu, "'Not a Cute Fashion Accessory': Gucci's $800 'Indy Full Turban' Draws Backlash," *Washington Post*, May 16, 2019, https://www.washingtonpost.com/nation/2019/05/16/nordstroms-indy-full-turban-gucci-draws-sikh-protests/.

12. Anoop Bhogal-Nair and Mona Moufahim, "We Asked Sikh Men in Britain What the Turban Means to Them—Here's What They Told Us," *Conversation* (blog), April 14, 2023, http://theconversation.com/we-asked-sikh-men-in-britain-what-the-turban-means-to-them-heres-what-they-told-us-202781.

13. Obi Anyanwu and Tonya Blazio-Licorish, "How Cultural Appropriation Became a Hot-Button Issue for Fashion," *Women's Wear Daily* (blog), November 3, 2020, https://wwd.com/feature/how-cultural-appropriation-became-a-hot-button-issue-for-fashion-1234579968/.

14. Helen Murphy, "Selma Blair Hits Back at Accusations of Cultural Appropriation After Posting Headwrap Picture," *People Magazine*, May 30, 2019, https://people.com/movies/selma-blair-cultural-appropriation-accusations-head-wrap/.

15. Prinzivalli, "Selma Blair Is Being Accused of Cultural Appropriation for Wearing a Turban."

16. Murphy, "Selma Blair Hits Back at Accusations of Cultural Appropriation After Posting Headwrap Picture."

17. Laura Berlinsky-Schine and Deanna deBara, "What Is Cultural Appropriation? 22 Examples to Know in 2023," *Fairygodboss*, October 17, 2023, https://fairygodboss.com/career-topics/cultural-appropriation.

18. Andrew Griffin, "Met Gala 2018: Angry Catholics and Conservatives Accuse Organisers of 'Religious Appropriation' over Theme," *Independent*, May 8, 2018, https://www.independent.co.uk/news/world/americas/met-gala-2018-theme-catholic-rihanna-pope-heavenly-bodies-a8340846.html.

19. Rebecca Tuvel, "Putting the Appropriator Back in Cultural Appropriation," *British Journal of Aesthetics* 61, no. 3 (July 1, 2021): 361, https://doi.org/10.1093/aesthj/ayab010.

20. C. Thi Nguyen and Matthew Strohl, "Cultural Appropriation and the Intimacy of Groups," *Philosophical Studies* 176, no. 4 (April 1, 2019): 987, https://doi.org/10.1007/s11098-018-1223-3.

21. Thi Nguyen and Strohl, "Cultural Appropriation and the Intimacy of Groups," 987.

22. Brigitte Vézina, *Curbing Cultural Appropriation in the Fashion Industry* (Waterloo: Centre for International Governance Innovation, 2019), 11, https://www.cigionline.org/sites/default/files/documents/paper%20no.213.pdf.

23. Julie Valk, "The 'Kimono Wednesday' Protests: Identity Politics and How the Kimono Became More than Japanese," *Asian Ethnology* 74, no. 2 (2015): 380.

24. Seph Rodney, "The Confused Thinking Behind the Kimono Protests at the Boston Museum of Fine Arts," *Hyperallergic*, July 17, 2015, http://hyperallergic.com/223047/the-confused-thinking-behind-the-kimono-protests-at-the-boston-museum-of-fine-arts/.

25. "Boston Kimono Exhibit in Race Row," Trending, *BBC News*, July 8, 2015, https://www.bbc.com/news/blogs-trending-33450391.

26. Greg Cook, "MFA Director on Kimono Controversy: 'I Think That Was Misguided and Apologize,'" WBUR, February 8, 2016, https://www.wbur.org/news/2016/02/08/mfa-kimono-controversy.

27. Valk, "The 'Kimono Wednesday' Protests," 385, 386.

28. Valk, "The 'Kimono Wednesday' Protests," 394; Charlotte Brill, "Wearing Kimono—Appropriation or Appreciation?," *Medium* (blog), April 9, 2021, https://charlotte-brill.medium.com/wearing-kimono-appropriation-or-appreciation-a93dd099355b.

29. Stephanie McFeeters, "Counter-Protesters Join Kimono Fray at MFA," *Boston Globe*, July 18, 2015, https://www.bostonglobe.com/arts/2015/07/18/counter-protesters-join-kimono-fray-mfa/ZgVWiT3yIZSlQgxCghAOFM/story.html, cited in Valk, "The 'Kimono Wednesday' Protests."

30. Cook, "MFA Director on Kimono Controversy."

31. Brill, "Wearing Kimono"; Asia Ryan, "Too Sensitive or Too Ignorant? The Rise of Political Correctness in the US," *Mesa Press* (blog), November 13, 2021, https://www.mesapress.com/opinion/2021/11/13/too-sensitive-or-too-ignorant-the-rise-of-political-correctness-in-the-us/.

32. Annette Martín, "What Is White Ignorance?," *Philosophical Quarterly* 71, no. 4 (September 1, 2021): pqaa073, https://doi.org/10.1093/pq/pqaa073.

33. Marzia Milazzo, "On White Ignorance, White Shame, and Other Pitfalls in Critical Philosophy of Race," *Journal of Applied Philosophy* 34, no. 4 (2017): 559, https://doi.org/10.1111/japp.12230.

34. Charles W. Mills, "White Ignorance," in *Race and Epistemologies of Ignorance*, ed. Shannon Sullivan and Nancy Tuana (Albany: SUNY Press, 2012), 21.

Chapter 4

1. Erich Hatala Matthes, "Cultural Appropriation and Oppression," *Philosophical Studies* 176, no. 4 (April 1, 2019): 1006, https://doi.org/10.1007/s11098-018-1224-2.
2. Amy Allen, "Feminist Perspectives on Power," in *The Stanford Encyclopedia of Philosophy*, ed. Edward N. Zalta and Uri Nodelman (Stanford, CA: Metaphysics Research Lab, Stanford University, 2022), https://plato.stanford.edu/archives/fall2022/entries/feminist-power/.
3. Maeve McKeown, "Structural Injustice," *Philosophy Compass* 16, no. 7 (2021): 2, https://doi.org/10.1111/phc3.12757.
4. Iris Marion Young, *Responsibility for Justice* (New York: Oxford University Press, 2011), 52, https://doi.org/10.1093/acprof:oso/9780195392388.001.0001.
5. Jonathan Wolff and Avner de-Shalit, *Disadvantage* (Oxford: Oxford University Press, 2007).
6. Matthes, "Cultural Appropriation and Oppression," 1003.
7. Denise Cuthbert, "Beg, Borrow or Steal: The Politics of Cultural Appropriation," *Postcolonial Studies: Culture, Politics, Economy* (July 1, 1998): 258, https://doi.org/10.1080/13688799890174.
8. Mathias Siems, "The Law and Ethics of 'Cultural Appropriation,'" *International Journal of Law in Context* 15, no. 4 (December 2019): 417, https://doi.org/10.1017/S1744552319000405.
9. Siems, "The Law and Ethics of 'Cultural Appropriation,'" 417; Dianne Lalonde, "Does Cultural Appropriation Cause Harm?," *Politics, Groups, and Identities* 9, no. 2 (March 15, 2021): 331, https://doi.org/10.1080/21565503.2019.1674160.
10. Andrea N. Walsh and Dominic McIver Lopes, "Objects of Appropriation," in *The Ethics of Cultural Appropriation*, ed. James O. Young and Conrad G. Brunk (Hoboken, NJ: Blackwell Publishing, 2009), 225, 226.
11. Rebecca Tuvel, "Putting the Appropriator Back in Cultural Appropriation," *British Journal of Aesthetics* 61, no. 3 (July 1, 2021): 366, https://doi.org/10.1093/aesthj/ayab010 (emphasis in original).
12. Janice Gassam Asare, "How Hair Discrimination Affects Black Women at Work," *Harvard Business Review*, May 10, 2023, https://hbr.org/2023/05/how-hair-discrimination-affects-black-women-at-work.
13. Lauren Cochrane, "Kylie Jenner's Cornrows and the Racial Politics of Hair," Fashion, *Guardian*, July 13, 2015, https://www.theguardian.com/fashion/shortcuts/2015/jul/13/kylie-jenner-cornrows-racial-politics-hair.
14. Nicole Whitney, "A Dilemma of Cultural Appropriation in Fashion," *Medium* (blog), December 3, 2016, https://medium.com/@nicoleawhitney94/a-dilemma-of-cultural-appropriation-in-fashion-6bc743b2d6e6.

15. Faith Karimi, "Blackfishing: Here's What It Is and Why People Are Doing It," CNN, July 8, 2021, https://www.cnn.com/2021/07/08/entertainment/blackfishing-explainer-trnd/index.html.
16. Lalonde, "Does Cultural Appropriation Cause Harm?," 331.
17. John Rowell, "The Politics of Cultural Appropriation," *Journal of Value Inquiry* 29, no. 1 (1995): 138.
18. Matthes, "Cultural Appropriation and Oppression," 1005.
19. Lalonde, "Does Cultural Appropriation Cause Harm?," 37.
20. There is vigorous philosophical dispute on the subject of what exploitation is specifically. For an overview, see Alan Wertheimer, "Exploitation," Stanford Encyclopedia of Philosophy, October 3, 2022, http://plato.stanford.edu/entries/exploitation/.
21. Ben Westhoff, "Pop Appropriation: Why Hip-Hop Loves Eminem but Loathes Iggy Azalea," Music, *Guardian*, February 11, 2015, https://www.theguardian.com/music/2015/feb/11/hip-hop-appropriation-eminem-iggy-azalea.
22. Mona Kosar Abdi et al., "White Hip-Hop Artists Navigate Line Between Art and Cultural Appropriation," *ABC News*, July 22, 2023, https://abcnews.go.com/Entertainment/white-hip-hop-artists-navigate-line-art-cultural/story?id=101550759.
23. Kerra L. Bolton, "Eminem, a Rare White Artist Speaks Out for His Black Fans," CNN, October 11, 2017, https://www.cnn.com/2017/10/11/opinions/eminem-trump-clash-opinion-bolton/index.html.
24. Professor of cognitive science (and one of the author's neighbors) Jim Davies proposed an alternative interpretation. Perhaps, he suggested, rap music actually *is* part of Eminem's culture. In a private communication to me, Davies wrote, "He grew up around it, doing it, with lots of black people around him. He was surrounded by it growing up, just like the black people around him. He was enculturated into rap similarly to how the black kids around him were. He just happens to be recognizably white by race, but maybe not by culture." He therefore asks, "Could someone make an argument that the music of Em's culture is rap music, and that he's not borrowing anything?" This interpretation also seems reasonable, and highlights the complicated ways in which race and culture do and do not overlap.
25. Mia Baeza, "Iggy Azalea's Cultural Appropriation Controversies," *Medium* (blog), September 25, 2023, https://medium.com/@miabaeza2005/iggy-azaleas-cultural-appropriation-controversies-93958a07b054.
26. N'dea Yancey-Bragg, "Fashion Designer Balenciaga Accused of Cultural Appropriation over $1,190 Sweatpants," *USA Today*, September 13, 2021, https://www.usatoday.com/story/life/fashion/2021/09/13/balenciaga-racist

-sweatpants-cultural-appropriation-accusations/8320213002/; Niko Koppel, "Are Your Jeans Sagging? Go Directly to Jail," Fashion, *New York Times*, August 30, 2007, https://www.nytimes.com/2007/08/30/fashion/30baggy.html.

27. Gene Demby, "Sagging Pants and the Long History of 'Dangerous' Street Fashion," Code Switch, NPR, September 11, 2014, https://www.npr.org/sections/codeswitch/2014/09/11/347143588/sagging-pants-and-the-long-history-of-dangerous-street-fashion.

28. Haroon Siddique, "US Town Bans Saggy Pants," World News, *Guardian*, June 14, 2007, https://www.theguardian.com/world/2007/jun/14/usa.haroonsiddique.

29. Demby, "Sagging Pants and the Long History of 'Dangerous' Street Fashion."

30. Kelsie Smith, "For 13 Years, This City Banned Saggy Pants. Now, Officials Have Voted to Repeal the Law," CNN, September 11, 2020, https://www.cnn.com/2020/09/11/us/florida-saggy-pants-ban-trnd/index.html.

31. Lalonde, "Does Cultural Appropriation Cause Harm?," 337.

32. "Jamie Oliver's 'Jerk Rice' Accused of Cultural Appropriation," *BBC News*, August 20, 2018, https://www.bbc.com/news/newsbeat-45246009.

33. Zoe Williams, "Here's the Main Issue Behind the Jamie Oliver Jerk Rice Row—and It's Not Cultural Appropriation," Opinion, *Guardian*, August 22, 2018, https://www.theguardian.com/commentisfree/2018/aug/22/heres-the-main-issue-behind-the-jamie-oliver-jerk-rice-row-and-its-not-cultural-appropriation.

34. "Jamie Oliver's 'Jerk Rice' Accused of Cultural Appropriation."

35. Williams, "Here's the Main Issue Behind the Jamie Oliver Jerk Rice Row."

36. Lalonde, "Does Cultural Appropriation Cause Harm?," 337.

37. Elizabeth Roberts, "Chanel's $1,325 Boomerang Condemned as 'Cultural Appropriation,'" CNN, May 16, 2017, https://www.cnn.com/style/article/chanel-boomerang/index.html.

Chapter 5

1. Olúfẹ́mi O. Táíwò, *Reconsidering Reparations* (New York: Oxford University Press, 2022), 41–42.

2. Patrick Wolfe, "Settler Colonialism and the Elimination of the Native," *Journal of Genocide Research* 8, no. 4 (December 1, 2006): 387–409, https://doi.org/10.1080/14623520601056240; Yann Allard-Tremblay and Elaine Coburn, "The Flying Heads of Settler Colonialism; or the Ideological Erasures of Indigenous Peoples in Political Theorizing," *Political Studies* 71, no. 2 (May 1, 2023): 359–378, https://doi.org/10.1177/00323217211018127.

3. Allard-Tremblay and Coburn, "The Flying Heads of Settler Colonialism," 362, 363.

4. Elisa Novic, *The Concept of Cultural Genocide: An International Law Perspective* (Oxford: Oxford University Press, 2016).

5. Dennis Zotigh, "Native Perspectives on the 40th Anniversary of the American Indian Religious Freedom Act," *Smithsonian Magazine*, November 30, 2018, http://www.smithsonianmag.com/blogs/national-museum-american-indian/2018/11/30/native-perspectives-american-indian-religious-freedom-act/.

6. Bob Joseph, *21 Things You May Not Know about the Indian Act* (Port Coquitlam, BC: Indigenous Relations Press, 2018).

7. Lenard Monkman, "How a Historical Ban on Spirituality Is Still Felt by Indigenous Women Today," CBC, March 25, 2017, https://www.cbc.ca/news/indigenous/historical-ban-spirituality-felt-indigenous-women-today-1.4036528.

8. Will Kymlicka, *Multicultural Citizenship: A Liberal Theory of Minority Rights* (Oxford: Oxford University Press, 1996).

9. Jeff Corntassel, "Re-Envisioning Resurgence: Indigenous Pathways to Decolonization and Sustainable Self-Determination," *Decolonization: Indigeneity, Education & Society* 1, no. 1 (2012): 86–101; Leanne Betasamosake Simpson, "Indigenous Resurgence and Co-Resistance," *Critical Ethnic Studies* 2, no. 2 (2016): 19–34, https://doi.org/10.5749/jcritethnstud.2.2.0019.

10. Catherine Lu, *Justice and Reconciliation in World Politics* (Cambridge: Cambridge University Press, 2017).

11. Kris Inwood and Evan Roberts, "'Indians Are the Majority of the Prisoners'? Historical Variations in Incarceration Rates for Indigenous Women and Men in British Columbia," *Howard Journal of Crime and Justice* 59, no. 3 (2020): 350–369, https://doi.org/10.1111/hojo.12381; Vicki Chartrand, "Unsettled Times: Indigenous Incarceration and the Links Between Colonialism and the Penitentiary in Canada," *Canadian Journal of Criminology and Criminal Justice* 61, no. 3 (July 2019): 67–89, https://doi.org/10.3138/cjccj.2018-0029; Laurence J. Kirmayer and Gregory Brass, "Addressing Global Health Disparities Among Indigenous Peoples," *Lancet* 388, no. 10040 (July 9, 2016): 105–106, https://doi.org/10.1016/S0140-6736(16)30194-5; T. Kue Young et al., "Disparities Amidst Plenty: A Health Portrait of Indigenous Peoples in Circumpolar Regions," *International Journal of Circumpolar Health* 79, no. 1 (January 1, 2020): 1805254, https://doi.org/10.1080/22423982.2020.1805254.

12. United Nations, "United Nations Declaration on the Rights of Indigenous Peoples," September 13, 2007, https://www.un.org/development/desa/indigenouspeoples/wp-content/uploads/sites/19/2018/11/UNDRIP_E_web.pdf.

13. Patti Tamara Lenard and Peter Balint, "What Is (the Wrong of) Cultural Appropriation?," *Ethnicities* 20, no. 2 (2020): 336.
14. Wolf Depner, "Growing Residential School Denial 'the Last Step in Genocide': Report," *Terrace Standard*, June 20, 2023, https://www.terracestandard.com/news/growing-residential-school-denial-the-last-step-in-genocide-report/.
15. Nudrat Karim, "Dreamcatchers Are Not Your 'Aesthetic,'" *Indigenous Foundation* (blog), n.d., https://www.theindigenousfoundation.org/articles/dreamcatchers.
16. Moira Wyton, "Residential School Denialists Tried to Dig Up Suspected Unmarked Graves in Kamloops, B.C., Report Finds," *CBC News*, June 17, 2023, https://www.cbc.ca/news/canada/british-columbia/denialists-tried-to-access-unmarked-gravesite-tkemlups-report-1.6879980.
17. Kishan Lara-Cooper and Sammy Cooper, "'My Culture Is Not a Costume': The Influence of Stereotypes on Children in Middle Childhood," *Wicazo Sa Review* 31, no. 2 (2016): 56–68, https://doi.org/10.5749/wicazosareview.31.2.0056; Anh Ly and Lynden Crowshoe, "'Stereotypes Are Reality': Addressing Stereotyping in Canadian Aboriginal Medical Education," *Medical Education* 49, no. 6 (2015): 612–622, https://doi.org/10.1111/medu.12725.
18. Karim, "Dreamcatchers Are Not Your 'Aesthetic.'"
19. Shaina Willison, "An Artifact of Colonialism: The Canadian Government's Obligation to Assist Indigenous Repatriation Efforts," *McGill International Review*, March 31, 2022, https://www.mironline.ca/an-artifact-of-colonialism-the-canadian-governments-obligation-to-assist-indigenous-repatriation-efforts/. Controversy around the return of objects is not limited to Indigenous or other colonized peoples, of course. The United Kingdom persists in refusing to return the Greek Elgin Marbles to the Parthenon in Athens, from where they were taken; former British prime minister Rishi Sunak recently described them as a "huge asset" to the United Kingdom, explaining that the United Kingdom has "cared for" the Elgin Marbles for generations. See Aubrey Allegretti, "No Plans to Return Parthenon Marbles to Greece, Says Rishi Sunak," Art and Design, *Guardian*, March 13, 2023, https://www.theguardian.com/artanddesign/2023/mar/13/no-plans-to-return-parthenon-elgin-marbles-to-greece-says-rishi-sunak.
20. Jaela Bernstien, "Canada's Museums Are Slowly Starting to Return Indigenous Artifacts," *Macleans*, June 22, 2021, https://macleans.ca/culture/canadas-museums-are-slowly-starting-to-return-indigenous-artifacts/.
21. Truth and Reconciliation Commission of Canada, "Calls to Action," 2015, https://nctr.ca/records/reports/, https://nctr.ca/records/reports/.

22. Another strategy is for museums that preserve and display Indigenous artifacts to collaborate with Indigenous Peoples to ensure that displays are properly respectful of Indigenous culture. We consider this solution in chapter 6.
23. "Manchester Museum to Return Aboriginal Artefacts in Special Ceremony," Manchester, *BBC News*, September 5, 2023, https://www.bbc.com/news/uk-england-manchester-66709623.
24. Ben Knight, "Karl May Museum Hangs On to Native American Scalp," DW, February 2, 2016, https://www.dw.com/en/karl-may-museum-hangs-on-to-native-american-scalp/a-19020100.
25. Brenda Haas, "Karl May Museum Returns Native American Human Scalp," DW, April 13, 2021, https://www.dw.com/en/karl-may-museum-returns-native-american-human-scalp/a-57181103.
26. Lisa Michelle King, "Revisiting Winnetou: The Karl May Museum, Cultural Appropriation, and Indigenous Self-Representation," *Studies in American Indian Literatures* 28, no. 2 (2016): 40, 27, https://doi.org/10.5250/studamerindilite.28.2.0025.
27. Tawnya Plain Eagle, "Millions of Indigenous Artifacts Are Still on Display in Museums Around Canada," CBC, June 2, 2023, https://www.cbc.ca/television/millions-of-indigenous-artifacts-are-still-on-display-in-museums-around-canada-1.6863670.
28. Alana Sayers, "Cultural Appropriation of First Nations Art," *AGGV Magazine*, March 1, 2018, https://emagazine.aggv.ca/cultural-appropriation-first-nations-art/.
29. Chelsey Luger, "5 Ways to Spot Indigenous Cultural Appropriation in Wellness Culture," *Self*, November 30, 2022, https://www.self.com/story/indigenous-cultural-appropriation.
30. Jill Ettinger, "The Complicated Ethics of Burning Sage and Smudging: Is It Cultural Appropriation?," *Ethos* (blog), October 3, 2022, https://the-ethos.co/burn-sage-bundles-cultural-appropriation/.
31. Ashley Tibbits, "This Indigenous Practice Will Purify Your Mind, Body, and Spirit," *Zoe Report*, November 30, 2022, https://www.thezoereport.com/wellness/native-american-sweat-lodge.
32. Barbara Fraser, "The Perils and Privileges of an Amazonian Hallucinogen," *Sapiens*, August 3, 2017, https://www.sapiens.org/culture/ayahuasca-tourism-amazon/.
33. Ocean Malandra, "Why You Should Think Twice Before Booking an Ayahuasca Retreat," *Matador Network*, July 25, 2022, https://matadornetwork.com/read/ayahuasca-retreat-ethics/.

34. Mark Hay, "The Colonization of the Ayahuasca Experience," *JSTOR Daily*, November 4, 2020, https://daily.jstor.org/the-colonization-of-the-ayahuasca-experience/. For an examination of the place of ayahuasca in Indigenous culture, see Evgenia Fotiou, "The Globalization of Ayahuasca Shamanism and the Erasure of Indigenous Shamanism," *Anthropology of Consciousness* (Fall 2016): 151–179.

35. Ann Babe, "Ayahuasca Tourism Is Ripping Off Indigenous Amazonians," *Vice* (blog), May 10, 2016, https://www.vice.com/en/article/qbn8vq/ayahuasca-tourism-is-ripping-off-indigenous-amazonians.

36. Babe, "Ayahuasca Tourism Is Ripping Off Indigenous Amazonians."

37. Perhaps if the health benefits of these practices were significant—equivalent, say, to curing cancer—then there would be additional reasons to encourage or even require "appropriation." But that does not appear to be the case in the examples considered here.

38. Babe, "Ayahuasca Tourism Is Ripping Off Indigenous Amazonians."

39. Malandra, "Why You Should Think Twice Before Booking an Ayahuasca Retreat."

40. Hay, "The Colonization of the Ayahuasca Experience."

41. Kelly Hearn, "The Dark Side of Ayahuasca," *Men's Journal*, December 4, 2017, https://www.mensjournal.com/travel/the-dark-side-of-ayahuasca-20130215; Fraser, "The Perils and Privileges of an Amazonian Hallucinogen."

42. Francesca Fionda, "Fake Art Hurts Indigenous Artists as Appropriators Profit," *Discourse*, November 30, 2018, https://thediscourse.ca/urban-nation/fake-art-indigenous.

43. Solen Roth, Eva Lange, and Joanne Kienholz, "Aboriginal-Themed Giftware Market in Major Vancouver Tourism Sites" (Association for Tropical Biology and Conservation, October 2010); Fionda, "Fake Art Hurts Indigenous Artists as Appropriators Profit."

44. Fionda, "Fake Art Hurts Indigenous Artists as Appropriators Profit."

45. "Fake Art Harms Culture Campaign," Indigenous Art Code, 2016, https://indigenousartcode.org/news-article/fake-art-harms-culture-campaign.

46. "Reclaim Indigenous Arts," Reclaim Indigenous Arts, 2018, https://www.reclaimindigenousarts.com/home.

47. Willow Fiddler, "Norval Morriseau's Family Speaks Out About Controversial Toronto Artist," *APTN News* (blog), May 9, 2017, https://www.aptnnews.ca/national-news/norval-morriseaus-family-speaks-out-about-controversial-toronto-artist/; Joanna Lavoie, "Leslieville Gallery Cancels Art Show over Concerns of Indigenous Cultural Appropriation," Toronto.com, April 27, 2017,

https://www.toronto.com/things-to-do/leslieville-gallery-cancels-art-show-over-concerns-of-indigenous-cultural-appropriation/article_ecfd4923-880d-5d2a-a06c-a4617c2fadc3.html.

48. Alexander Nazaryan, "White Painter Loses Art Show over Cultural Appropriation Debate," *Newsweek*, May 5, 2017, https://www.newsweek.com/cultural-appropriation-outcry-succeeds-cancelling-gallery-show-white-painter-594924.

49. Shanifa Nasser, "Painter Inspired by Indigenous Art Accused of 'Cultural Genocide' as Gallery Cancels Show," CBC, April 28, 2017, https://www.cbc.ca/news/canada/toronto/toronto-gallery-indigenous-art-cancels-amandapl-1.4091529.

50. Micahel Tymchuk, "Open Letter Accuses Non-Indigenous Artist of Cultural Appropriation," CBC, December 8, 2017, https://www.cbc.ca/news/canada/british-columbia/newman-coleman-artists-open-letter-indigenous-appropriation-1.4437958.

51. Carey Newman, "An Open Letter to Sue Coleman from Members of the Indigenous Community," December 4, 2017, https://www.dropbox.com/s/xkd6rfmqr6nt9kn/An%20Open%20Letter%20to%20Sue%20Coleman-For%20Public%20Release.pdf?dl=0.

52. Philip Pettit, *Republicanism: A Theory of Freedom and Government* (Oxford: Oxford University Press, 1997).

53. Tymchuk, "Open Letter Accuses Non-Indigenous Artist of Cultural Appropriation."

54. Jean Teillet, "Opinion: There Is Nothing Innocent About the False Presumption of Indigenous Identity," *Globe and Mail*, November 11, 2022, https://www.theglobeandmail.com/opinion/article-there-is-nothing-innocent-about-the-false-presumption-of-indigenous/.

55. Kim TallBear, "Native 'Identity' Fraud Is Not Distraction, but the Final Indian Bounty," *Unsettle* (blog), March 27, 2022, https://kimtallbear.substack.com/p/native-identity-fraud-is-not-distraction.

56. Neegahnii Madeline Chakasim, "Pretendians and Their Impacts on Indigenous Communities," Indigenous Foundation, May 10, 2022, https://www.theindigenousfoundation.org/articles/pretendians-and-their-impacts-on-indigenous-communities; Jessica Kolopenuk, "The Pretendian Problem," *Canadian Journal of Political Science / Revue Canadienne de Science Politique* 56, no. 2 (June 2023): 468–473, https://doi.org/10.1017/S0008423923000239.

57. Teillet, "Opinion."

58. TallBear, "Native 'Identity' Fraud Is Not Distraction, but the Final Indian Bounty."

59. Elaine Coburn, ed., *More Will Sing Their Way to Freedom: Indigenous Resistance and Resurgence* (Halifax: Fernwood Publishing, 2015), 32.
60. Taiaiake Alfred and Jeff Corntassel, "Being Indigenous: Resurgences Against Contemporary Colonialism," *Government and Opposition* 40, no. 4 (January 2005): 608–609, https://doi.org/10.1111/j.1477-7053.2005.00166.x.

Chapter 6

1. Ronald Dworkin, "The Right to Ridicule," *New York Review of Books* 53, no. 5 (March 23, 2006).
2. Edwin J. Gasque, "Censorship in Art: Preserving Culture or Infringing on Freedom of Expression?," *Medium* (blog), July 28, 2023, https://medium.com/@gasqueedwin/censorship-in-art-preserving-culture-or-infringing-on-freedom-of-expression-115cdbc9568f.
3. Dianne Lalonde, "Does Cultural Appropriation Cause Harm?," *Politics, Groups, and Identities* 9, no. 2 (March 15, 2021): 342, https://doi.org/10.1080/21565503.2019.1674160.
4. Elizabeth Lapensée, "Video Games Encourage Indigenous Cultural Expression," NITV, April 20, 2017, https://www.sbs.com.au/nitv/article/video-games-encourage-indigenous-cultural-expression/dp7s20v9c.
5. Laura Hudson, "One Way to Avoid Cultural Appropriation: Seek Collaborators, Not Just Characters," Boing Boing, August 4, 2015, https://boingboing.net/2015/08/04/never-alone-game.html.
6. Lalonde, "Does Cultural Appropriation Cause Harm?," 342.
7. Joshua Williams, "Carla Fernandez, Ethically Engaging Indigenous Peoples," Fashion Consort, December 16, 2023, https://www.fashionconsort.com/fc-podcasts-news-network/feature-carla-fernandez-ethically-engaging-indigenous-peoples.
8. Eliza Jordan, "Carla Fernández and Pedro Reyes Are Preserving Mexican Culture," Whitewall, November 1, 2023, https://whitewall.art/lifestyle/carla-fernandez-and-pedro-reyes/.
9. Brigitte Vézina, *Curbing Cultural Appropriation in the Fashion Industry* (Waterloo: Centre for International Governance Innovation, 2019), 13, https://www.cigionline.org/sites/default/files/documents/paper%20no.213.pdf.
10. Elizabeth Raiss, "A Poetic Vision," *Suited Magazine*, 2018, https://suitedmagazine.com/archives/2018/06/13/a-poetic-vision/. This example is perhaps an easy case in the sense that there was a clear "recipient" for the financial benefit that Metsavaht was offering. In others, identifying "which community" or "who" should receive this benefit may well be subject to the difficulties we outlined earlier of knowing who speaks for a community, and therefore who

should receive and dispense this benefit on a community's behalf. Thanks to Jim Davies for identifying this issue.

11. Ann-Marie Kennedy and Marian Makkar, "Cultural Appropriation," in *The Sage Handbook of Marketing Ethics*, ed. Lynne Eagle et al. (Thousand Oaks, CA: Sage Publications, 2020), 164, https://researchrepository.rmit.edu.au/esploro/outputs/bookChapter/Cultural-Appropriation/9921982384701341.

12. Government of Panama, "Special System for the Collective Intellectual Property Rights of Indigenous Peoples," WIPO, 2000, https://www.wipo.int/wipolex/en/text/177308.

13. James Anaya, "The Status of Indigenous Peoples' Rights in Panama," United Nations General Assembly, July 3, 2014, https://un.arizona.edu/sites/default/files/2021-11/UNSR_JA_Country_Visit_Panama_2014_English.pdf.

14. "Indian Arts and Crafts Act of 1990," US Department of the Interior, 1990, https://www.doi.gov/iacb/act#:~:text=The%20Indian%20Arts%20and%20Crafts%20Act%20(IACA)%20of%201990%20(,products%20within%20the%20United%20States.

15. Jemima Gravatt, "The Indian Arts and Crafts Act of 1990: Fit for Purpose?," Center for Art Law, November 8, 2023, https://itsartlaw.org/2023/11/08/the-indian-arts-and-crafts-act-of-1990-fit-for-purpose/.

16. Elaine Velie, "Artist Who Faked Native Identity Gets 18-Month Sentence," *Hyperallergic*, May 22, 2023, http://hyperallergic.com/823457/artist-jerry-chris-van-dyke-faked-native-identity-gets-18-month-sentence/.

17. Acee Agoyo, "Fake Indian Art Still a Major Problem Despite Federal Responsibilities," *Indianz.Com* (blog), March 14, 2023, https://indianz.com/News/2023/03/14/fake-indian-art-still-a-major-problem-despite-federal-responsibilities/.

18. Mathias Siems, "The Law and Ethics of 'Cultural Appropriation,'" *International Journal of Law in Context* 15, no. 4 (December 2019), https://doi.org/10.1017/S1744552319000405.

19. Sari Sharoni, "The Mark of a Culture: The Efficacy and Propriety of Using Trademark Law to Deter Cultural Appropriation," *Federal Circuit Bar Journal* 26, no. 3 (2017): 436.

20. Nicky Woolf, "Urban Outfitters Settles with Navajo Nation After Illegally Using Tribe's Name," US News, *Guardian*, November 19, 2016, https://www.theguardian.com/us-news/2016/nov/18/urban-outfitters-navajo-nation-settlement.

21. Siems, "The Law and Ethics of 'Cultural Appropriation,'" 412.

22. A. W. Eaton and Ivan Gaskell, "Do Subaltern Artifacts Belong in Art Museums?," in *The Ethics of Cultural Appropriation*, ed. James O. Young and

Conrad G. Bruno (Hoboken, NJ: John Wiley & Sons, 2009), 243, https://doi.org/10.1002/9781444311099.ch10.

23. Truth and Reconciliation Commission of Canada, "Calls to Action," 2015, https://nctr.ca/records/reports/, https://nctr.ca/records/reports/.

24. Andrea N. Walsh and Dominic McIver Lopes, "Objects of Appropriation," in *The Ethics of Cultural Appropriation*, ed. James O. Young and Conrad G. Brunk (Hoboken, NJ: Blackwell Publishing, 2009), 225.

25. "France Returns 26 Looted Artifacts and Artworks to Benin," Reuters, November 12, 2021, https://www.cnn.com/style/article/benin-art-returned-scli-intl/index.html.

26. Jonny Walfisz, "Should European Museums Return African Heritage Items?," *Euronews*, July 15, 2022, https://www.euronews.com/culture/2022/07/15/should-european-museums-return-african-heritage-items.

27. Brittany Hobson, "National Museum Changes Stance on Genocide, Sides with Inquiry Findings," *APTN News* (blog), June 6, 2019, https://www.aptnnews.ca/national-news/national-museum-changes-stance-on-genocide-sides-with-inquiry-findings/.

28. Nosmot Gbadamosi, "Stealing Africa: How Britain Looted the Continent's Art," Al Jazeera, October 12, 2021, https://www.aljazeera.com/features/2021/10/12/stealing-africa-how-britain-looted-the-continents-art.

29. Canadian Museums Association, *More than Giving Back: Repatriation Toolkit* (Canadian Museums Association, 2022), 16, https://museums.ca/uploaded/web/TRC_2022/More-than-giving-back.pdf.

30. Smithsonian Center for Folklife and Cultural Heritage, "Shared Stewardship of Collections," 2019, https://folklife-media.si.edu/docs/folklife/Shared-Stewardship.pdf.

31. Eaton and Gaskell, "Do Subaltern Artifacts Belong in Art Museums?," 250.

32. John Rowell, "The Politics of Cultural Appropriation," *Journal of Value Inquiry* 29, no. 1 (1995): 137.

33. Rowell, "The Politics of Cultural Appropriation," 142.

34. "Cultural Appropriation and the Canada Council's Approach," Canada Council for the Arts, accessed May 3, 2024, https://canadacouncil.ca/funding/funding-decisions/decision-making-process/application-assessment/context-briefs/cultural-appropriation.

35. "Frightening Attack on the Imagination," letters to the editor, *Globe and Mail*, March 28, 1992.

36. Andrea Fatona, "'Where Outreach Meets Outrage': Racial Equity at the Canada Council for the Arts (1989–1999)" (PhD diss., University of Toronto,

2011), 168, https://central.bac-lac.gc.ca/.item?id=NR78179&op=pdf&app=Library&is_thesis=1&oclc_number=1019461488.

37. Janice Hladki, "Problematizing the Issue of Cultural Appropriation," *Alternate Routes: A Journal of Critical Social Research* 11 (1994): 106.

38. "Cultural Appropriation and the Canada Council's Approach."

Conclusion

1. Peter Balint and Patti Tamara Lenard, *Debating Multiculturalism: Should There Be Minority Rights?* (Oxford: Oxford University Press, 2022).

FURTHER READING

Cultural Appropriation and Cancel Culture

Castle, Jeremiah. "New Fronts in the Culture Wars? Religion, Partisanship, and Polarization on Religious Liberty and Transgender Rights in the United States." *American Politics Research* 47, no. 3 (May 1, 2019): 650–679. https://doi.org/10.1177/1532673X18818169.

Chiamaka, Ezedimbu, Emeka Agba, and Femi Olufunmilade. "Cultural Appropriation and Cancel Culture: A Global Survey." *Global Partners in Education Journal* 10, no. 2 (December 13, 2022): 84–93.

DeGroot, Christopher. "The Case for Cultural Appropriation: A Polemic Against Political Correctness." *New English Review*, April 2018. https://www.newenglishreview.org/articles/the-case-for-cultural-appropriation-a-polemic-against-political-correctness/?print=print.

Cultural Appropriation and Consumption

Hogans, Kristian, and Laura McAndrews. "Away from Violence Toward Justice: A Content Analysis of Cultural Appropriation Claims from 2013–2020." *Fashion Practice* 15, no. 3 (September 29, 2022): 493–517. https://www.tandfonline.com/doi/full/10.1080/17569370.2022.2118333.

Kennedy, Ann-Marie, and Marian Makkar. "Cultural Appropriation." In *The Sage Handbook of Marketing Ethics*, edited by Lynne Eagle, Charles R. Taylor, Patrick De Pelsmacker, and Stephan Dahl, 155–168. Thousand Oaks, CA: Sage Publications, 2020. https://researchrepository.rmit.edu.au/esploro/outputs/bookChapter/Cultural-Appropriation/9921982384701341.

Lin, Jason D., Nicole You Jeung Kim, Esther Uduehi, and Anat Keinan. "Culture for Sale: Unpacking Consumer Perceptions of Cultural Appropriation." *Journal of Consumer Research* 51, no. 3 (October 2024): 571–594. https://doi.org/10.1093/jcr/ucad076.

Norris, Pippa. "Cancel Culture: Myth or Reality?" *Political Studies* 71, no. 1 (February 1, 2023): 145–174. https://doi.org/10.1177/00323217211037023.

Cultural Appropriation in General

Jackson, Jason Baird. "On Cultural Appropriation." *Journal of Folklore Research* 58, no. 1 (April 2021): 77–122. https://doi.org/10.2979/jfolkrese.58.1.04.

Lalonde, Dianne. "Does Cultural Appropriation Cause Harm?" *Politics, Groups, and Identities* 9, no. 2 (March 15, 2021): 329–346. https://doi.org/10.1080/21565503.2019.1674160.

Lenard, Patti Tamara, and Peter Balint. "What Is (the Wrong of) Cultural Appropriation?" *Ethnicities* 20, no. 2 (2020): 331–352.

Matthes, Erich Hatala. "Cultural Appropriation and Oppression." *Philosophical Studies* 176, no. 4 (April 1, 2019): 1003–1013. https://doi.org/10.1007/s11098-018-1224-2.

Matthes, Erich Hatala. "Cultural Appropriation Without Cultural Essentialism?" *Social Theory and Practice* 42, no. 2 (2016): 343–366.

Reed, Trevor G. "Fair Use as Cultural Appropriation." *California Law Review* 109, no. 4 (2021): 1373–1442.

Young, James O. *Cultural Appropriation and the Arts*. Hoboken, NJ: John Wiley & Sons, 2010.

Young, James O. "Should White Men Play the Blues?" *Journal of Value Inquiry* 28, no. 3 (1994): 415–424.

Indigenous Peoples and Cultural Appropriation

Coleman, Elizabeth Burns. *Aboriginal Art, Identity and Appropriation*. London: Routledge, 2005. https://doi.org/10.4324/9781315263526.

Fotiou, Evgenia. "The Globalization of Ayahuasca Shamanism and the Erasure of Indigenous Shamanism." *Anthropology of Consciousness* (Fall 2016): 151–179.

King, Lisa Michelle. "Revisiting Winnetou: The Karl May Museum, Cultural Appropriation, and Indigenous Self-Representation." *Studies in American Indian Literatures* 28, no. 2 (2016): 25–55. https://doi.org/10.5250/studamerindilite.28.2.0025.

Kramvig, Britt, and Anne Britt Flemmen. "Turbulent Indigenous Objects: Controversies Around Cultural Appropriation and Recognition of Difference." *Journal of Material Culture* 24, no. 1 (March 1, 2019): 64–82. https://doi.org/10.1177/1359183518782719.

Lara-Cooper, Kishan, and Sammy Cooper. "'My Culture Is Not a Costume': The Influence of Stereotypes on Children in Middle Childhood." *Wicazo Sa Review* 31, no. 2 (2016): 56–68. https://doi.org/10.5749/wicazosareview.31.2.0056.

Ng, Wendy, Syrus Marcus Ware, and Alyssa Greenberg. "Activating Diversity and Inclusion: A Blueprint for Museum Educators as Allies and Change Makers." *Journal of Museum Education* 42, no. 2 (April 3, 2017): 142–154. https://doi.org/10.1080/10598650.2017.1306664.

Riley, Angela R., and Kristen A. Carpenter. "Owning Red: A Theory of Indian (Cultural) Appropriation." *Texas Law Review* 94, no. 5 (April 25, 2016): 859–931.

Museum Practices and Cultural Artifacts

Appiah, Kwame Anthony. "Whose Culture Is It, Anyway?" In *Cultural Heritage Issues: The Legacy of Conquest, Colonization and Commerce*, edited by James A. R. Nafziger and Ann Nicgorski, 207–221. Leiden: Brill, 2009.

Bukan, Umbrin. "To Accurately Portray Histories, Museums Need to Do More than 'Reimagine' Galleries." *Conversation*, September 13, 2022. http://theconversation.com/to-accurately-portray-histories-museums-need-to-do-more-than-reimagine-galleries-189109.

Eaton, A. W., and Ivan Gaskell. "Do Subaltern Artifacts Belong in Art Museums?" In *The Ethics of Cultural Appropriation*, edited by James O. Young and Conrad G. Bruno, 235–267. Hoboken, NJ: John Wiley & Sons, 2009. https://doi.org/10.1002/9781444311099.ch10.

Grafton, Emily, and Julia Peristerakis. "Decolonizing Museological Practices at the Canadian Museum for Human Rights." In *Indigenous Notions of Ownership and Libraries, Archives and Museums*, edited by Camille Callison, Loriene Roy, and Gretchen Alice LeCheminant, 229–243. Berlin: De Gruyter, 2016. https://doi.org/10.1515/9783110363234-018.

INDEX

PATTI TAMARA LENARD is Professor of Ethics in the Graduate School of Public and International Affairs, University of Ottawa. She is the author of *Democracy and Exclusion; Trust, Democracy, and Multicultural Challenges*; and *How Should Democracies Fight Terrorism?*, and coauthor of *Debating Multiculturalism* and *Ordinary People, Extraordinary Actions: Refuge Through Activism at Ottawa's St. Joe's Parish*. In Ottawa, she runs a community organization called Rainbow Haven, which sponsors, settles, and advocates for 2SLGBTQI+ refugees: https://www.facebook.com/rainbowhavenottawa/.

PETER BALINT was Associate Professor in International & Political Studies at University of New South Wales Canberra, and convenor of the International Ethics Research Group. He was a political theorist whose research centered on the issues of diversity and of privacy in the information age. He is the author of *Respecting Toleration: Traditional Liberalism & Contemporary Diversity* (which was highly commended by the APSA Crisp Prize panel in 2018), the coauthor of *Debating Multiculturalism*, and the coeditor of *Liberal Multiculturalism and the Fair Terms of Integration*. He was regularly asked to consult government on issues of migration, multiculturalism, and citizenship. He was a founding member of the Global Justice Network and founding editor of its journal, *Global Justice: Theory Practice Rhetoric*.

Publisher contact:
The MIT Press
Massachusetts Institute of Technology
77 Massachusetts Avenue, Cambridge, MA 02139
mitpress.mit.edu

EU Authorised Representative:
Easy Access System Europe, Mustamäe tee 50,
10621 Tallinn, Estonia
gpsr.requests@easproject.com

Printed by Integrated Books International,
United States of America